ZERO ^{TO}_A MILLION
IN ONE YEAR!

The Entrepreneur's Guide To Overnight Success

DR. BEN LERNER

Zero to a Million in One Year:
The Entrepreneur's Guide to Overnight Success

by Dr. Ben Lerner

Trade paperback ISBN: 978-1-943294-53-4
Ebook ISBN: 978-1-943294-54-1

Cover design by Martijn van Tilborgh

Zero to a Million in One Year is also available on Amazon Kindle, Barnes & Noble Nook and Apple iBooks.

CONTENTS

INTRODUCTION

HERE ARE THE INDUSTRIES in which I have started companies that I've been able to innovate, market, and build to a million in a year.

1. Licensing
2. Franchising
3. Publishing and writing
4. Product sales, retail
5. Product sales, wholesale
6. Technology
7. Lab testing
8. Manufacturing
9. Health care–specifically chiropractic care
10. Real estate

My first two books were *New York Times* bestsellers, and in the health and fitness industry I've been able to quickly create plans, processes, and promotions for businesses and services I've owned or offered in a part-time capacity, in a very crowded marketplace. All in all, I have started more than 20 businesses and the goal is always to get up and running and get to that million dollar mark fast; usually in a year. I have tried a few things out that have been outside of my zone of expertise and have failed to get off of the ground. However, with any well-chosen, mission-based business zero to one million in a year has been a consistent target I have been able to hit.

The same strategies helped me to create Holy Grail-type partnerships with professional and Olympic sports teams, major corporations, megachurches, government, schools, and school systems.

What I really believe gives me the most to offer and inspired me to write this particular book was the industry that has been my focus—wellness. My first book was published by Thomas Nelson, then the world's largest publisher of Christian books. They published my book *Body by God* at the same time they published Dave Ramsey's *Total Money Makeover*. Mr. Ramsey and I did some television appearances and speaking engagements together at the time, so I was able to gauge the public's desire for a book about being healthy against one about money. As you might imagine, when you watched the crowd respond to a talk about getting out of debt and becoming rich and one about why it's so important to cut carbs and go organic, there was no comparison.

The point I'm making, however, is that both our books went on to become *New York Times* bestsellers. I was able to reach a few million dollars in sales of my first book in a year, even though no one really wanted it. When I look at companies like Dunkin' Donuts or Papa John's, I think, "Of course they can sell a whole lot of product, they sell flour with either sugar or cheese and tomato sauce. That's easy—I'm selling lima beans!"

If you're looking to grow fast, you can use the resources here to gain velocity whether you're selling something everyone wants and nobody really needs–like a donut or pizza—or something few people want but everybody really needs, like fitness and chiropractic.

- My first chiropractic office was generating seven times the profession average in only three months. Within three years I had five of them doing as much as 20 times the average!

- In the gym business, I created the 1990s version of a marketing funnel using the Yellow Pages instead of the Internet to explode my business.

- In publishing, I had two *New York Times* bestsellers with my first two books. After five books we started self-publishing and sold just as many, but cut out the middleman.

- As a real estate investor, I saw $1 million in profits on my first deal, and more than $1 million on my second.

- Product manufacturing, wholesaling and retailing–my channel- and program-based process quickly reached $9 million a year.

- I turned the clinic, book, and product model into a multimillion-dollar-per-year, multiple-unit owner-ship, franchising, and licensing business.

Where neither my mom or dad nor their parents before them had ever seen $1 million, I had over a million in savings and was debt-free by my mid-twenties. I did not know what I was doing at the beginning, so the first lesson for a Zero to a Million business is, "Just get going." I'm certain there are current and former employees, contractors, and partners who might say, "Wait, why are you writing the book? I did this part or that part." If you did, thank you—but I knew to hire you, partner with you, lead you, and, in some cases, part ways with you at the right time to build the many Zero to a Million businesses I have had.

Eventually I did learn everything about running and managing these businesses too. Some of that was by trial and error and some by going back to school or through certifications to advance my degrees and training. Getting my Master's in Industrial and Organizational Psychology was particularly helpful in hiring, training, and building a culture. With online colleges, anyone can advance their education and training while still continuing to work and spend time with their family.

I did also learn from the school of hard knocks. I want to teach you about whether or not to have a partner and, if you do, where the landmines are buried. Please don't make my mistakes with partners! It is also critical you learn what authoritarian and transactional leadership is, where it is beneficial, how to apply it, and where it is important to add supportive and transformational leadership principles in order to build a productive but also healthy culture. I used to be a Russian Czar of a boss and it got results in terms of metrics, but it was not much of a blessing to my team members. A mission-based business should be of benefit to all and the end result should be a fun, thriving culture. Real success comes when you serve your team first!

VELOCITY COACHING

Each of you should use whatever gift you have received to serve others, as faithful stewards of God's grace in its various forms. —1 Peter 4:10

There is a term called "Escape velocity." This is the velocity necessary to break free from gravitational attraction for a rocket moving into space. It is calculated by the equation U_g (the universal gravitational constant) $- Gm_1m_2/r$ (mass of the planet, star, or other body), and commonly described as the speed needed to "break free."

The Bible says that God gives us the desires of our hearts (Ps. 37:4). If you're breathing, God still has a big plan for you and He's likely given you something important that you desire to do. This book and my work in the company I founded, Velocity Coaching and Consulting is about how to take your work from desire to thriving reality in the shortest period of time—to escape from the earth's atmospheric pressures that stop our purpose from going into orbit. Enclosed in this book and in the coaching we provide are not only the steps to go from Zero to a Million fast but also to set yourself up for the beyond so you're not just a one-hit wonder. It is about changing the world.

At the core of the concept is the mission-based business. God has given us an assignment and, just like a mid-term paper, God forbid we don't complete the assignment. I don't want an "F" from God. The saddest words are, "What might have been." Most people die with their music still in them, stuck in a job, so I want you to grow with a mission. Mission is more powerful than work and more impactful; it's your big part of a big God who has called you to do big things. What I have experienced personally and through coaching, counseling, mentoring, and consulting is that the impact you can make in work gets multiplied when that work becomes a mission.

MISSION ADDS A ZERO

I will go before you and will level the mountains; I will break down gates of bronze and cut through bars of iron.
—Isaiah 45:2

Let's look at the mindset of "adding a zero." If you are capable of a $10,000-a-year business, but you are on mission, then God can add a zero and make that a $100,000-a-year business If you are capable of getting to $100,000 in one year, then your mission-based business is capable of adding a zero and becoming a $1 million business. People add to a business. They can go from 100 to 200 to 300 by adding 100 at a time. But, God multiplies a mission-based business. You can go from 100 to 10,000 to 1,000,000 if instead of adding 100 you multiply by 100. See that difference? Where addition gets you to 300, multiplication gets you to a million. Just do the math—learn the value of a mission-based business and live by multiplication rather than addition.

Nothing is more certain than the failure of the one who quits and the success of the man who never will.

Chapter 1

WHAT IS YOUR MISSION?

Meditate on my word day and night, observe to do according to all that is written therein: for then thou shalt make thy way prosperous, and then thou shalt have good success. - Joshua 1:8 (emphasis added)

THIS BIBLE VERSE has an important message for all of us entrepreneurs looking for best practices: focus on His word 24/7/365 and you'll not only succeed, you will have something God describes as "good success" (Josh. 1:8, KJV/NKJV).

First of all, it is important to notice that *if there is such a thing as good success, then there can be a bad success.* That point is not too hard to make. After all, there are plenty of really successful drug dealers, porn site operators, politicians, cigarette manufacturers, junk food producers, and men and women who cheat on their spouses—the list goes on. Consequently, becoming a super-successful, multimillion-dollar-producing Christian entrepreneur requires making certain which success type you are pursuing.

Defining what is good success can be tough. With mission, however, where we see the word *good*, we remove an "o" and make it *God*. If you measure good success as to whether or not it is God success, then you're off to a decent start. You can pull off a good idea (with two o's), but you'll often find yourself out there without God and, like Sysiphus, pushing the rock uphill only to find it back at the bottom the next day, and having to start all over again.

I once had very successful client who just had that special something. He glowed and he managed to work glorifying God into every conversation. I asked him to what he attributed his strong spiritual focus, his peace, and his success, and he said, "Results." He continued, "I feel like I am a pretty smart guy and can make many things happen. However, God is moving billions of puzzle pieces around and knows a whole lot more than me about how to put them together in the best way possible for my ultimate good. I can do things on my own, but my ideas just never bear the kind of fruit that a God idea can."

You don't just want good ideas, you want God ideas. For the purpose of this book, I'll call "good success" the results you experience on your mission, or to quote Elwood Blues, on your "mission from God."

A mission from God is a foolproof plan because, as former President of the Czech Republic, Vaclav Havel, said, *"Work for something because it is God, not just because it stands a chance to succeed."* Good success still comes with hard work, ups and downs, some desperate times, staff turnover, and customer complaints. Luke 17:1 says, "Things that cause people to stumble are bound to come." There's going to be stuff, but when you really feel God's pleasure at your attention to the cause you've been given, it is like the soreness you get the day after a work-out—it hurts, but you have the satisfaction and fulfillment of knowing that you've accomplished something good.

When I traveled with the U.S. World Greco-Roman Wrestling Team to Sweden for the World Championships as a team doctor, I found out that good morning there was spelled "God morning." It is God's morning—and afternoon, and evening. Your business is also God's business if you want to have God success. God success does good. Ultimately a mission, even if it's lawn care or furniture manufacturing, results in bringing others into alignment with God for His glory, and for the blessing of people and His planet. If you do, He's behind that.

When you align your work with your calling you get a high-voltage anointing. In alignment, we can rely on the age-old Christian fact that for every vision there is provision. It is often said that there is no such thing as financial security, but there is the safety of mission. During presidential elections, down economies, and bear markets I've often been comforted by Jeremiah 17:7-8:

> "This is what the Lord says: But blessed is the man who trusts in the Lord, whose confidence is in him.
>
> He will be like a tree planted by the water
>   that sends out its roots by the stream.
> It does not fear when heat comes;
>   its leaves are always green.
> It has no worries in a year of drought
>   and never fails to bear fruit."

The circumstances, conditions, and the seasons of the world do not pertain to a man or woman doing God work. With superior, supernatural guidance and resources, you just are not as bound by the physical realities of the planet as other people. In fact, for you every day is harvest day. With a high-voltage anointing, there is no waiting for the right season. Don't live by natural principles, or get natural results. Live by spiritual principles and get supernatural results. Again, this doesn't take away from struggles, it just takes away a feeling of hopelessness or being overwhelmed while you go through them and gives you a peace that surpasses understanding because you know, "If God is for you, who (or what) can come against you" (Rom. 8:31). You even change the principles of math, as I have noted: if you're capable of 10, with God you end up at 100, 1,000, or millions. Supernatural success!

Another interesting factoid about the God-work anointing is how you will be treated and the doors that will open. On a mission, you will see treatment at airport, hotels, restaurants, businesses, and churches change. They will start making exceptions to the rules to work with you. Your kids will become more favored at school. God doesn't send you out on an assignment without first going in front of you. He gets there first and wins the ultimate battle for you, as has been demonstrated in many parts of the Bible. Just ask Gideon, Joshua at Jericho, and King Jehoshaphat. You'll fail, you'll trip, and you might even fall—but you'll fall forward. We're told, "Though a righteous man fall seven times, he will rise again… and again and again" (Prov. 24:16).

To any entrepreneur: if you want to do it, do it now. If you don't, you're going to regret it. —Catherine Cook, cofounder of MyYearbook.

While most people choose their college by location, level of education, reputation, costs, or the quality of the parties, I chose mine by wrestling team. Sure, they had a good pre-med program and I originally wanted to be an orthopedist, but mostly they had a world-class head coach, Olympian assistant coaches, and many athletes vying for an Olympic berth. Unfortunately, I spent more time with the trainer for treatment of injuries than with my elite coaches and teammates. But it did not take away from my desire to make it to the world stage. I wanted to figure out how to be part of the U.S. wrestling performance team and their chiropractor. I ended up being the first official chiropractor to work and travel with the U.S. wrestling teams in 1995 at the world championships and at the 1996 Olympics—my first of four Olympics. How did I do it? Hopefully you've guessed: mission.

I was actually part of a plan to serve U.S. athletes training and living at the Olympic Training Center in Colorado Springs, Colorado. Most of these athletes live like paupers. They are the training poor, living with many roommates, pennies to their name, and dependent on the small stipends from the affiliated governing body of their sport, along with the goodwill of others. I went out to Colorado to help the International Fitness Professionals Association certify the athletes as personal trainers and show them how to build a business. While there, I ran into several of my college wrestling buddies who I found could really use my help with their physical health and training. They introduced me to the U.S. coaching staff and the rest is wrestling history.

If you just work on stuff that you like and you're passionate about, you don't have to have a master plan with how things will play out. —Mark Zuckerberg, founder of Facebook.

MISSION DESCRIPTION

Achieve a purpose, complete your assignment, fulfill a destiny, win your race, fight for a cause, do what God created you to do. These are just some of the ways to describe what should be the business you are engaged in. Please do not miss the point on this one. Not everyone was born to be a pastor, or a missionary, or to lead a not-for-profit company geared towards humanitarian efforts. The majority of great entrepreneurs have not achieved success specifically in a religious endeavor. I've known restaurateurs, hoteliers, landscaper company owners, financial advisors, online product sales providers, and many, many other business owners and service providers who have built tremendously popular and lucrative businesses and are using their resources, connections, and experiences to find lasting fulfillment, serve God, support and grow the Christian community, or change lives through their generous philanthropic efforts, on an impressive scale. A vast majority of towns and cities around the world have a local salon, gym, or franchise owner who has transformed the moral and ethical culture and united the region to do good work.

Because of my corporate success, I'm able to have success in what the Bible calls us to do—feed, clothe, and house the poor. Sitting at the table with me when I'm at meetings for organizations like Coalition for the Homeless in Orlando, are guess what, very few ministers or ministries, but rather people that lead mission-based businesses. They know that you don't make money for yourself, you make it for the mission–you make it to do good work and to glorify God. The result is way more money than you can make for yourself.

The literal million-dollar question then is, "What is your assignment, race, purpose, destiny, God-given thing to do?" What is the cause worth giving your whole life to?

The answer to that question provides comfort and the potential for peace in good times and bad. Regardless of the economy or who the current president is, on a mission from God you'll have the faith to know all things are working together for your good, and to be able to say, "If God is for me, who can stand against me?"

It's not about ideas. It's about making ideas happen.
—Scott Belsky, co-founder of Behance.

UNIDIRECTIONAL FOCUS

When everything seems to be going against you, remember that the airplane takes off against the wind, not with it.
—Henry Ford, founder of Ford Motor Company.

Sitting in a local Christian men's meeting called Iron Men of God, we had the opportunity to hear from a former Green Beret who now serves God by saving children from the grips of sex trafficking. I learned that there is a heated rivalry between Green Berets and Navy SEALS. The speaker wanted us to be clear that while SEALS have a "hell week," to become a Green Beret you have to survive 21 days of Special Forces Assessment and Selection (SFAS).

He said that in order to get through these three weeks of abuse that are specifically designed to break you and get you to quit, you have to be unidirectionally focused. Apparently, there were many guys bigger, more talented, stronger, and in better shape than he was, but he committed to himself that, "I'm going to either make it through or they are going to put my stiff, cold body in a bag and throw it in the back of a truck." A bit extreme, yes, but extreme situations call for extreme commitment. If you're going to prepare yourself to overcome the battles a successful leader has to face and win the wars God has set before you, then unidirectional commitments must be made: all-in, never surrender, and no retreat. If you are in say, "Hooyah!" This is the military response to the mission, meaning, "Heard, understood, and acknowledged," or in other words, "All in!"

World-renowned educator and author Leonard Sweet shares a story in one of my books, *Winning My Race,* that illustrates unidirectional focus really well. At 7:00 p.m., on October 20, 1968, a few thousand spectators remained in the Mexico City Olympic Stadium. It was cool and dark. More than an hour earlier, Mamo Wolde of Ethiopia, looking as fresh as when he started the race, crossed the finish line, the winner of the 26-mile, 385-yard event. As the remaining spectators prepared to leave, they heard the sound of sirens and police whistles. A lone figure wearing number 36 and the colors of Tanzania entered the stadium. His name was John Stephen Akhwari. He was the last man to finish the marathon. He had fallen during the race and injured his knee and ankle. Now, with his leg bloodied and bandaged, he grimaced with each hobbling step around the 400 meter track. The spectators rose and applauded him. After crossing the finish line, Akhwari slowly walked off the field. A reporter later asked him, "Why did you continue the race after you were so badly injured?" He replied, "My country did not send me 7,000 miles to start the race. They sent me 7,000 miles to finish it."

Every Christian is commissioned to "run the race that is marked out for us" (Heb. 12:1). Throughout the centuries, since Christ first challenged His first disciples to go out and fulfill the Great Commission, men and women have chosen to run their individual races until they crossed heaven's finish line. It is important for every Christian to understand that they are not to run someone else's race, or spend their life competing against another Christian. Each race or *mission* is marked out uniquely for them. In essence, we do not create the race that we are to run; Christ designs the track for us.

Scripture states that God will take us from "glory to glory" (2 Cor. 3:18). Glory to glory means we are getting better and better and moving closer and closer to who we have been called to become. You take little people steps towards God and He takes bigger God steps towards you. But as the legendary Christian motivator Jim Rohn used to say, "If you don't move, He don't move." Move and be certain that Christ has won for us the victory (John 16:33).

Through mission, we are ideally suited to find the Christlike potential in each of our chosen spheres of life, which we were designed to influence. If God has called you to win your race, no matter what winning is for you, God-forbid you don't win it. We have to believe we've found our life's purpose and be unidirectionally focused in order to persevere, mature, stay in hope, keep the faith, and inspire others. Then it is a foregone conclusion that we will achieve that purpose—that we will have not only run the race, not only finished the race, but will have won the race.

GOOD NEWS: YOUR MISSION IS NOT A NEEDLE IN A HAYSTACK

I have the original seven-foot movie poster from *Rocky* with the tag-line at the bottom that reads, "His whole life was a million-to-one shot." The movie is the epic tale of man living in the hood, uneducated, and breaking thumbs on the dock for the mob to make a living. A guy with nothing going for him and that nobody outside of his pet turtles, Cuff and Link, seemed to like. Yet, greatness, hope, and a glorious future awaited. By taking advantage of the opportunities that were presented to him, getting up early, eating raw eggs, punching frozen filet mignon, getting a good coach, and going to work every day, a million-to-one shot at fulfilling his destiny became one out of one.

I have worked with tens of thousands of actual and potential entrepreneurs and the question "What is my mission?" is probably the hardest to answer. After all, how do you truly know that you're doing exactly what God called you to do? While it would have been far more convenient to be born with a sticky note attached to your forehead from God that says "Lawyer," "accountant," "kid's ministry," "soccer player," or "Mother raising seven children," there are clues for all of us.

For me, the story was in two pretty easy-to-read chapters. In Chapter One, I was always worried about my parents. Their lifestyle was terrible and as a result they struggled with problems such as high cholesterol, high blood pressure, aches, pains, and fatigue. This pushed me to get into health, fitness, and psychology. In Chapter Two, when I was a teenager attempting to become an elite college wrestler and perhaps make a world or Olympic team like many of my teammates, my body really fell apart. I tore, pulled, or damaged my shoulders, ankles, knees, and back, and my digestive tract became ulcerated due to all of the anti-inflammatory drugs I was being given in order to keep me competing. At the ripe old age of 19, I was ready to throw in the towel when I was introduced to natural health care.

Through nutrition, chiropractic, better training methods, and getting off my medications my life was radically transformed. I went from a teenager with diagnosed arthritis, poor immunity, a herniated disc, and a bleeding ulcer to the picture of health and an All-American. As a result, I had a very big story to tell and was ready to change the world. The experience led me to get degrees and training in all of the areas that had helped me and find great satisfaction and good success in recreating the same story for others.

Many areas of work can fall under the heading of m*ission or purpose. The tough part, however, can be recognizing or discovering what you've been call to do.* A great way to look at and figure out whether or not work is mission and heading you towards not only personal reward but in fact, God success, is to determine the impact it has made on your own life.

Outside of health, my entrepreneurial passion was born out of my parents' struggles as well. My dad's was an incredible rags to riches story. He grew up in a gang, living on the streets of New York. Eventually, he became the first college graduate in his family and had his picture in the *Wall Street Journal* as the youngest vice president in a big Fortune 500 company. Sadly, the technology age wiped him out. There was no such thing as a computer when he went to school and started his career. With thousands of young men and women coming out of school who understood the computer the age, he was eventually let go and replaced. This moved me to want to be my own boss and never fall behind the times.

Pay attention to pains, challenges, and mayhem. These may be your maps. My family's issues with bosses, employment, finances, their mental and physical health along with my aches and pains really drove me to health care as well as wanting to learn business. It was and still is essential to me to fully understand what is required to launch and effectively manage your own company rather than work for someone else. My father's downsizing has made me a lifelong learner. I'm always getting that next degree or certification to make sure I stay ahead of the game. These areas of life became my mission. I found the "Why that made me cry." The roadmap of my family and personal life experiences, good and bad, has started me down a path and the journey continues.

In the Tom Cruise movie The Samurai, Katsumoto the samurai says to Cruise's character, Algren, "Do you believe a man can change his destiny?" Algren replies, "I believe a man does what he can until his destiny is revealed." The Bible says something similar, "Your word is a lamp to my feet and a light to my path" (Ps 119:105). The whole journey, the whole map, is not lit up but the next steps or, your feet, are. Your family, your own experiences, passions, likes, dislikes, and the needs you know need filling in the world are right there in front of you. Make a plan to get started and get moving towards your mission. Do what you can and God will reveal an ever-developing, ever-expanding mission to you.

A mission is not a needle in a haystack. It is not that difficult. It is not like the concept of there being only one man or woman in the whole world for you. God doesn't make it a million-to-one shot. He would not set up the world so that hardly anyone ever found the man or woman of their dreams or rarely discovered their destiny. He says, "If you seek me *you will* find me." You'll have hope and a future (Jer 29:11). So get seeking.

Remember, "The one who calls you is faithful, and he will do it" (1 Thess. 5:24).

Make sure you get your stars out. —J.D. Salinger.

FANTASY EXERCISE

Imagine you are going to be honored for an achievement in your chosen field. You will be given an award of Successful Achievement at a national convention. The convention hosts will introduce you and speak about you prior to your acceptance of your award. Write their introduction and speech honoring you. Include all your prior accomplishments, training, experience. Write out all the qualities and attributes you would like them to mention. Write what exactly you did that you are being honored for. What are your stars? What would you like them to be? What would you like to be remembered for? Just for a few minutes, be as great as you can be!

THE WHY FACTOR

"You have to have a why that makes you cry." Meaning, it has to be so connected to your heart that it moves you to tears.

Finding why:

- Why are we doing what we are doing?

- What do we hope to achieve?

- What purpose are we fulfilling?

An intention can be thought of as a goal. Other synonyms for the word intention include "purpose," "aim," "aspiration," and "resolve." Clear intentions hold tremendous creative power. In the areas of personal growth, relationships, career, and life choices, clarity of intention is an indispensable tool for achieving what we envision.

You need to find your compelling *why* and then put some urgency behind it. Find the compelling *why* that will inspire you and get you into immediate and consistent action. Your compelling why must have a deadline—for example: On [X months from today] I will have achieved X. On [X months from today] I will have completed X.

Philippians 3:13-14 says, "Brothers and sisters, I do not consider myself yet to have taken hold of it. But one thing I do: Forgetting what is behind and straining toward what is ahead, I press on toward the goal to win the prize for which God has called me heavenward in Christ Jesus."

THE 4 PRINCIPLES OF MISSION

Going from a job to a mission-based business

After getting my nutrition degree, I assumed that with my passion and healthy lifestyle my new nutrition practice would just take off. Yet, at the end of my first few months I had no business at all. I had produced zero. Even if you add a zero, it's now 00.

As a new grad, and without rich parents, I was broke My car would break down at every stoplight or sign. I had to learn a trick whereby I would open my door, push my little VW Scirocco with both feet until I got momentum and then use my right foot to pop the clutch. In order to make actual money, I had to work nights at my parents' convenience store. One of my fellow workers was a single mother of two in an absolutely terrifying state of health. She was only two years older than I was, in her early twenties, but she could easily pass for being as old as my mom. Much of this could be explained by her diet of convenience store hot dogs that probably contained used rat parts, candy bars, and the two Dr. Peppers she drank at every shift.

Her eating habits and subsequent cataclysmic healthy always prompted a plea from me to come see me in my clinical nutrition practice. Yet, as bad off as she was, I was unable to procure her as my client. I struck out with her just as I had with everyone else.

One day my co-worker's her six-year-old daughter informed me that her mom always has "my-rains" (migraines). Her mom confirmed that, yes, she spent her days in a dark room and her nights at work on tons of drugs, getting through shifts so she could make a buck. I told her, "That's it, you're coming into the clinic even if I had to pay for it!" It wasn't my clinic so it actually cost me $10 a visit to see her. But little did I know, it would be a dynamic shift towards being mission-based that would change my future.

This isn't one of my health books, but to make a long story short, every problem she had went away and she got off all of her drugs after completing a nutrition program and receiving chiropractic care. Every one. For this book, the area to focus on is that I ended up with more business than I could handle. I'm not saying it's a good idea to give away your services or pay for people to be your client, patient, or customer. What changed was the condition of my heart.

As soon as I approached my work from a community perspective–moms and dads out there suffering, leaving small children to fend for themselves while the parents slept in dark rooms–everything changed. Suddenly, I couldn't keep the actual paying business away. Giving, loving, and serving first and letting the opportunities and the money come as a consequence shifted me from having a job to being part of a mission-based business. It was a transition that changed my entire future.

There are four principles that make a mission-based business:

Principle #1: It's not your business.

I was trying to build my business, and as a result, it was written all over my face. While in my mind I was there for a purpose, my heart was for the purpose of Ben–to make more money, to be able to boast about a big practice, and to improve my transportation situation. "Whatever you do, work at it with your whole being, for the Lord and not for men,."

Principle #2: It's about people.

If you're saying you're sent to serve God, then it's not only God's business, it's God's people too. You are third: it's God, people, then you. Therefore, love your neighbor more than yourself.

Principle #3: People are attracted to a group bigger than them and a purpose greater than theirs.

If you follow principles one and two, then your magnet becomes strong. Others become attracted to those that are making a difference through serving a mission in their communities. Big people are not inspired by a small vision.

Principle #4: Serve and let the money take care of itself.

I don't believe the scripture "The worker is worth his wages" (1 Tim. 5:18) means you're entitled to a buck. What I have discovered is that when you focus on a vision, there is God's provision. Money is a mission side effect.

Mission has been proven to be better than a job. In their book *If it Ain't Broke...Break It!*, authors Robert J. Kriegel and Louis Patler cite a study of 1,500 people over twenty years that shows how passion makes a big difference.

The groups were divided into two. Group A was 83 percent of the total and chose a career based on making money now so they could do what they wanted in life in the future. Group B was the other 17 percent and they chose their careers based on the opposite; they chose based on what they were passionate about now and would concern themselves with money later.

The results after 20 years:

- 101 of the 1,500 became millionaires.

- Of the 101 millionaires, 100 were from Group B, those who had chosen to pursue their passions before money.

When I moved from my nutrition consulting job to a full-time job as a college graduate, I applied these four principles. I hate to say it was an overnight success, but it was an overnight success. I started getting six-figure commission checks every month—more money than I knew existed, at that time. Perhaps the most interesting part, I could care less. I was having the time of my life while pushing my car to work. Although I was able to buy a new one pretty quickly and never had to drive a beater again, fulfillment is not about finances. While my mother used to say, "Rich or poor, it's good to have money" or as someone else said, "The best way to help the poor is to not be one of them," let money be a side effect.

BUTT-PRINTS

A man is lying awake restlessly in his bed, contemplating his own pain and suffering and considering all of the terrible challenges in the world. Exhausted, he looks up at the ceiling of his bedroom and says out loud, "God, have you forgotten us?" Not hearing a response, he cries again, "God, do you even exist?"

When he finally sleeps, he has a dream. A dream so clear he thinks he is awake. He is looking down a long, sandy beach and notices at some points in his journey there were footprints. These were the times life was good, he was healthy, the economy was booming, and things were going well in the world. At other times, when his life was rough and the world was falling apart around him, he sees only the outline of what looks like a butt. They are "butt-prints."

So he asks God, "How come when things are going well, I see footprints and during the times everything is going bad—only butt-prints?"

"My son," He answers, "the times you saw footprints were the times when you were walking down the path that I had planned out for you."

"And the butt-prints, he queries

"That had nothing to do with me," God says. "That's when you were sitting on your a--."

We all know the passage from James (2:14, 26), "What good is it, my brothers and sisters, if someone claims to have faith but has no deeds? Show me your faith without deeds, and I will show you my faith by my deeds... As the body without the spirit is dead, so faith without deeds is dead." You've been given a mission and a vision from God. Proverbs 29:18 says, "Without a prophetic vision, my people perish." It is also said that without people, the vision from God perishes: we all have something to do. Now take your faith, get off your butt and let's go to work!

Chapter **2**

URGENCY: STRUCTURE, FUNCTION, AND EXECUTION

One man with courage makes a majority. —President Andrew Jackson.

THERE USED TO be an enormous sign near the inter-gate trams in the Atlanta airport that had a picture of Tiger Woods playing golf in the rain. The caption read, "Perfect conditions are rarely an option." Change, ambiguity, chaos, and turmoil have become the norm and those that can thrive in them will succeed. Those that point to them as excuses will likely fail.

Whether you believe God has called you to it or just see the work as a noble cause, the world comes with gravity in it. There is resistance against anything, including that which pleases God. Without resistance, our muscles don't grow–in fact, you cannot even survive without the forces of gravity.

You must be prepared for the challenges and moving at the speed of growth to succeed, no matter how great or spiritual the cause. Our plans for the future can't be encumbered by current realities.

URGENCY

The original Dow Jones Industrial was made up of 12 companies, including American Cotton Oil; American Sugar; American Tobaccos; Chicago Gas; Distilling & Cattle Feeding; General Electric (GE); North American; Tennessee Coal Iron and RR; U.S. Leather; and United States Rubber. Other than GE, the original companies selected as top in the world by Charles Dow in 1896 are all extinct.

According to one Harvard professor, it is the lack of urgency that continues to kill some of the largest (and smallest) companies in the world. A modest pace or full-out complacency can become an Ice Age for many, if not most businesses. In his book *Urgency*, Harvard Business School Professor John P. Kotter shares, "Urgent behavior is not driven by a belief that all is well or that everything is a mess, but instead, that the world contains great opportunities and great hazard." Urgency is a determination to get moving and start winning now—actually yesterday.

Look at Apple. They have won the technology race of this millennium by urgent innovation. While you are still happy with your current iPhone, they are urgently working on the next innovation so that before anyone can come up behind them and eat their cookie or you get even slightly bored, here comes the new iPhone or Apple product.

Urgently moving forward is not frenetic activity. In one of my most successful businesses, it became clear the team had grown complacent. We were very busy, so just getting through the day seemed like a noble effort and due great reward. However, I could smell the downturn. If you're not innovating, automating, creating, and creating momentum, there is an odor. That odor is the scent of your coming Ice Age–your extinction. Creating and keeping momentum takes urgency.

To help paint a picture of this for my staff, I began a team meeting by stacking five chairs, unstacking them, stacking them, unstacking them, and then stacking and unstacking them one more time for good measure. I shared with them that I was busy and working very hard, yet in the end, there were the chairs sitting right where they started. It was frenetic, hard work–but it was not getting me anywhere. Urgency is not crazy, it is a well thought out plan, executed in a very timely manner.

Kotter also observes that "change efforts most often fail when change agents did not create a high enough sense of urgency among enough people to set the stage for making a challenging leap in some new direction." It's good work done yesterday—despite what is often imperfect conditions.

Never give in–never, never, never, never, in nothing great or small, large or petty, never give in except to convictions of honour and good sense. Never yield to force; never yield to the apparently overwhelming might of the enemy.
—Winston Churchill, British Prime Minister.

STRUCTURE AND FUNCTION

Another business guru, Robert Fritz, points out that the difference between current reality and what it's built on and desired reality and what it's built on is the primary indicator of next-level success. The underlying structure of anything determines its behavior. In other words, you cannot build a high-rise building on the infrastructure of a two-bedroom, one-bathroom house. You may want to turn your lemonade stand into the Coca Cola Company, but it won't happen with the same mindset, skill-set, and infrastructure.

The will is subservient to the skill. You may really want something, but if you do not build, create, and acquire the skills then want will not turn into result it will turn into frustration.

There is an organizational structure called Lean Six Sigma. This approach works at the highest level and is critical to the budding entrepreneur or small to medium business. At its core the concept is to provide:

1. Top-level service.

2. Products and services truly valued by customers.

3. The lowest level of operating expenses.

Structurally, many companies provide products, services, and support the customer doesn't truly desire—as opposed to Steve Jobs, who gave you not only what you consciously desired, but what you didn't even know you wanted, but *really* wanted.

The urgent procedures have to be laid down across the right structures.

Steps to putting the right structures in place:

1. Introduce new procedures.

   a. Know the risk.

   b. Understand how it impacts all other parts of the organization.

   c. Success metrics–how will you very precisely know if the plan has been effective by goals being reached?

2. Innovations should not be reactive; reactive innovations often respond to complaints or crises, or knee-jerk reactions that are not taking the company into the future. This often turns into frenetic activity rather than progress.

3. Introduce innovations one at a time, so that you can measure impact without dilution.

4. Put a holistic, cohesive strategy to correct old, flat, or failing processes. Assess how new items can adversely affect one process while trying to fix another.

5. Metrics, metrics, metrics!

   a. Measuring and reacting to success or lack of it.

   b. Failing to continue driving continuous improvement.

   c. Plans and the team members that implement them are not measured through feeling and loyalty. They are measured and executives respond and refine based on whether or not these metrics are meeting agreed-upon expectations.

The path of least resistance: You have to take structural laws into account in order to succeed. If you lay new ideas on existing framework, they will always go back to the path of least resistance. —Robert Fritz.

SKILL BEATS WILL

A priest and a rabbi attended a boxing match together. Before the start of the first round, one of the fighters went through the Catholic practice of crossing himself. The rabbi asked the priest, "What is that for?" To which the priest replied, "It's not for nothing if the boy don't know how to fight!"

As we've been inferring, you can't manage what you can't measure. God gives us the desires of our heart, but we have to make sure we're not so heavenly minded that we're no earthly good. Getting the necessary education and training, and properly managing our organization will ultimately need to rise up to match your desire for a thing if the business is going to work.

Wherever your skill level and service delivery is at the start, to go from Zero to a Million and beyond it must be getting better. Set in your mind that you will build a culture of continual improvement. This means:

1. Create a code of standards.

2. Formulate process metrics that help you to continuously monitor performance and identify future improvement opportunities.

3. Don't change and grow for the sake of change and growth. Zero in on a system of continual feedback from your customers. Up to 50 percent of costs to support and deliver your product has been found to be

non-value-added work in the eyes of your customer. Without the right, consistent feedback most organizations only add value to the end product 5-10 percent of the time yet are continually raising their costs. This is *not a good formula!*

I have a powerful, praying wife. I defer to her prayers most of the time and generally live to regret it when I do not. On one occasion, however, my 10-year-old son's flag-football team was playing against the best team in the region. Most of the kids on my son's team had never played before and the opponent was a travel team with bigger, faster, more experienced athletes and had been beating teams by five or six touchdowns.

Our coach came up to my wife and I to tell us what we were up against that day and my wife said, "I strike losing in the name of Jesus. We're going to beat this team in Jesus' name!" While the coach and I both appreciated her positive, spiritual attitude very much, we also knew we'd have to trade that in for talent, skill, and experience if we were going to have a chance. On a positive note, we lost by only three touchdowns. Thank you, Jesus!

Areas of continual improvement for Lead Six Sigma:

1. Constantly improve consistency of service.

2. Constantly improve speed and efficiency of delivery.

3. Constantly build on trust.

4. Continuously reduce the cost of effectively and accurately executing on your business processes.

If an activity doesn't add value to the end product or adds time or steps without improving the product, then it's a waste!

URGENCY—THE FINAL STEP

The final step to effective urgency is execution. Ideas are easy, execution is a bear.

Billy Graham was once lost trying to find his way to a speaking engagement at a church. He stopped at the gas station to ask the attendant for directions. The attendant replied, "Pastor Graham, how are you going to tell me how to get to Heaven when you can't even find the church?" I'm fairly certain that was a joke and pre-GPS, but it makes a point: a big mission requires knowing how to get there. You can't save people if you don't know how to arrive at the office.

If you are a sports fan, then that means when your team loses consistently, you have called for the coach's head. I doubt any job lacks security like a professional or NCAA coach, but a leader in general is the job anyone is most likely to lose. Coaches, CEOs, and topline executives get fired way more often than the hourly wage earners that work for them.

If the team fails to win or the company does not grow or hit its goals, the blame generally goes straight up the food chain. Realistically, the issues are a failure to really know the team, the training and support required, the infrastructure, and the constraints—or, in other words what it takes to actually execute the plan. In Larry Bossidy and Ram Charan's book, Execution, they tell us the first building block of execution includes seven essential behaviors:

1. Know your people and your business.

2. Insist on realism.

3. Set clear goals and priorities.

4. Follow through.

5. Expand people's capabilities.

6. Know yourself.

FOCUS ON BEING THE BEST AND FORGET ABOUT THE REST

Finally, brothers, whatever is true, whatever is honorable, whatever is just, whatever is pure, whatever is lovely, whatever is commendable, if there is any excellence, if there is anything worthy of praise, think about these things (focus your eyes, dwell). — Phil. 4:8

The urgency, skills, structure, and plans to execute are the steps, but your power will be your ability to stay focused. Your focused state creates a spiritual charge or emotional valence that impacts everything you do. If you're going to start a mission and win it, then stay focused on the desires God has put in your heart and do not be deterred by a world that was created to distract you.

Most people awake to a drip feed of negativity from television, radio, the Internet, and all that is made available to them on their smartphone. Negativity and distraction becomes their dominant state.

Feelings link with thoughts and become your beliefs. Some people look in the mirror in the morning, decide they look old, and a thought bubble pops up that maybe they've lost a step, have run out of time, or will no longer accomplish the dreams they dreamed when they were younger. It is a whole lot of nonsense, but feelings and thoughts that fire together wire together and create patterns of behavior that can slow you down or stop you. If these connects are a disease, focus is the cure. You get to choose what gets your attention and the voice you associate with the feelings that pop up.

The goal is to get and stay on fire for your mission. When you are in a state of distraction, stress, or despair then the environment is moving or manipulating you. When you are on fire, on the other hand, fire defines every atmosphere it touches. Everything and everyone that comes into contact with fire is refined or verified. If situation, people, or cultures are not pure, they don't change the fire–fire changes them. If impurities exist they're smoked out.

There is another saying, "When you are on fire, everyone wants to come and watch you burn!" Focused, passionate people are a strong, attractive force in the universe and they dominate the room. Focused passion is influence and gives you a spiritual charge that influences everything and everyone around you.

The process of focusing is choosing what you'll read, listen to, and pay attention to each day and re-inserting the image of the future you want to create for your life. The Bible, specific passages, what excites you about your industry, the cause you are fighting for, and the vivid images of what your mission will look like when you succeed in the future should make up the morning and afternoon content you want to bathe your cells in. Hook yourself up to an IV. of what keeps you focused, passionate, and willing to ignore competition, circumstance, doubt, or haters.

The easiest way to sell yourself short is to compare your work to the competition. To say that you are 5% cheaper or have one or two features that stand out—this is a formula for slightly better mediocrity. —Seth Godin.

FROM PROSPECT TO PARTICIPANT TO PARTNER

Every business requires a conversion process. If you rely on charisma, luck, passion, or hope that prospective customers calling in or walking through the door will evolve into paying participants, then your chance of success drops precipitously.

There are four questions or objections someone is consciously or unconsciously voicing when they walk in the door. Your processes have to answer these questions or overcome these objections for people or they will never go from prospect to participant. This is uniquely true if the goal is not only a customer, but a bona fide member of the mission.

THE 4 QUESTIONS:

1. *Is it desirable?* You have to show them that the goal is well worth it.

2. *Is it even possible to achieve?* Your processes need to reveal to them that this is possible and share stories and testimonies that make it clear that the goal is achievable.

3. *Is that really the way?* Regardless of the value you provide, they have to come to understand that both the procedure

and the outcome are clearly appropriate and ecological in their particular situation.

4. Doubts to their worth, responsibility, and ability. They may not feel they are worthy of the product, result, or service. While they may feel a responsibility to their work or family, but they may believe they lack the capability to effectively utilize what you have to offer or follow through in order to make full use of it. Your processes must intentionally build self-esteem, and self-worth and help them clearly realize their mission obligations to others. What's more, the process has to be well supported and appear easy to pull off—or, as they say, "So easy a child can do it."

Start by doing what's necessary, then what's possible, and suddenly you are doing the impossible. —St. Francis of Assisi.

chapter **3**

BUILDING YOUR BUSINESS: GOING FROM MARKETING TO SAVING LIVES

There's lots of bad reasons to start a company. But there's only one good, legitimate reason, and I think you know what it is: it's to change the world.

—*Phil Libin, CEO of Evernote.*

To be a success in any sized mission, you need new patients, customers, franchisees, members, clients, buyers, and so on. This is generally THE challenge in any industry. I don't want to pour food dye on poop and call it playdough here. Today's world of marketing requires some technical know-how, content production, copy-writing talent, and consistency. I have had to familiarize myself and train my clients to engage in the many details of marketing and the many different forms required to create, sustain, and see results long-term. However, when you do this as part of a mission, once again you add a zero.

When it comes to marketing to the community, in a mission-based business, the term marketing is switched to "Saving lives outside." Isn't that what we're called to do–to save? If someone is drowning, they don't want you to offer them a product to change their life; they want it to save their life. It not only sounds more moral and spiritual, it is a better, socially conscious approach to gaining market share.

In high school and college, if I wasn't working out in a gym, I was also working as an employee of the gym. After graduation, I had really hoped I could create marketing relationships within the health clubs. I had also been a waiter for six years and the lifestyle of the restaurant business is really unhealthy. I envisioned really coming to the aid of waiters, bartenders, and managers that were up late, on their feet all of the time, eating dinner at 1 a.m., and always struggling with some pain or health problem. While working with gyms and restaurants was what I wanted, it was far from what I got.

Ready to market to the world, wearing a white shirt and red tie, and with my promotional flyer in hand, I walked into the first gym I could find. Before I could get a word out of my mouth, the front desk manager wearing a Bluto's Gym polo two sizes too small said, "If you're not a member here or looking for a membership, get out!" Demoralized, I got out.

Not wanting to quit too fast, and thinking maybe this approach worked better with restaurants, I went straight from there to a small Cuban cafe right across from our clinic on 27th and Sunset in Kendall, Florida. Still sporting my tie and holding my flyer, I walked in the front door and before getting a word out, someone I assumed to be the owner ran out from behind the counter, screaming something in Spanish

I could not understand. Holding a huge, butcher-looking knife, he chased me out the front door.

After arriving safely back in the Scirocco and double-checking for stab wounds, I was apoplectic. I became overwhelmed with dejection. Clearly, something was wrong with me. I questioned every decision I ever made in my life. Had I just wasted the last six years in college? Did I choose the wrong profession? Was there a God? If so, why did He love everyone else, but hate me?

As it turns out, it wasn't my calling that was off and certainly God has not singled one of us out to not love. What I needed was to apply the four Principles of the Mission-based Business to marketing. I realized it wasn't just me, it was my entire attitude, language, and approach to promoting my services that was that main problem.

Everyone has a mission that is important—even if they don't know it. If we're going to put our faith to work, somehow that has to bleed into promotion as well. Business building, or "marketing," has to be like the mission-based business itself. It has to be about serving and not just getting. When it comes to promotion, a friend in need is a real pain. However, a friend coming to help you expand your horizons is good news. I discovered that the key was switching from a promoting myself mindset to promoting others as a chance to support someone else's mission.

JOIN THE CO-MISSION

If you can bring your mission to someone else's mission you *co-mission*. When you co-mission, you trans-mission—you transcend what you each can do on your own, making a far grander difference than you could ever have done by yourselves.

THE CO-MISSION SCRIPT

I may sound like a glutton for punishment, but to try out my new vision for the co-mission I determined the best place to test this was at Bluto's Gym. While I hadn't got past the foyer before the Incredible Hulk tossed me from the premises, I figured that no restraining order had been issued so I was okay to give it one more shot.

I dislike marketing and confrontation as much as the next guy, so I was extremely nervous walking through the front door again. While this may sound like I've embellished the facts for the good of a movie, when I walked in the Hulk literally leaped over the desk and came running at me like I was there to steal one of his protein bars.

Before walking in the gym, I had written down key ways I could serve the gym's mission.

As soon as he reached me, index finger pointed at the door he was ready to shove me out of, I loudly proclaimed, "I want to see how I can help you save more lives!" This didn't stop him, but at least it stunned him for a second so I could get the first part of my offer out. I continued, "Your gym stops more heart disease and cancer than any doctor or hospital does. So I want to take care of the key managers for free and include you in my marketing efforts so we can reach more people and help our community."

To which he said, "No, get out." Not exactly the answer I was hoping for.

Genuinely confused and committed to making something work, I answered, "I'm not sure what you mean by no; I didn't ask you for anything?" There was a significant pause and for the first time since beginning my maiden voyage down the road of promotion, I saw the hard, impenetrable exterior of a potential partner crack. He finally replied, "I guess you're right, you didn't ask for anything."

I added the other areas I could help his gym. With my degree in nutrition, I could help the gym or support their nutrition staff through talks and consultations for members. I also added several other ways I could add value and help with growth and retention. This co-mission-based approach must have penetrated several inches of his generous cranium because he quickly called the owner over. We worked out the details, discussed opportunities, and they gave me a free membership to the gym. Together, Bluto's Gym and I took really good care of each other and the community doing many, many events together along with a whole lot of cross-referral.

WORKING IN THE COMMUNITY:

Your job is to serve–and nothing else. When entrepreneurs are struggling to get new business in from their community, there is a good chance that they're not doing anything to deserve it. Your job is to serve–period. Nothing more, nothing less. Go into organizations with a heart to serve, to take care of your community, and it will take care of you. While, yes, strategically you hope to gain from the relationship and ultimately there has to be fair exchange, you need to be sincerely pleased with the service you are providing.

A church I partnered with had me helping to unstack and stack chairs for the small, mobile services they had each week. After all, I had said to them, "I'm ready to serve you even if it means stacking chairs." To be perfectly candid, I had my doubts about my own sanity in being a chair-stacker. Yet, one Sunday they asked me to give the sermon to their 56 members (22, if you didn't include children and staff). I suppose as a result of seeing that my heart was to serve them and that I must really care about the church and its people if I was willing to be one of the chair guys, the power of co-missioning was strong that day. It was the only time I have ever spoken where 100 percent of the audience signed up to for my offer.

REMEMBER, I'M SELLING LIMA BEANS!

Keep in mind when I share these success stories that I'm not offering something people are generally waking up in the morning and deciding they really want. I use my wellness businesses as examples because they are the most difficult to sell. If it was pizza, donuts, Viagra, or how to get rich fast, then being on a mission isn't that important. Everyone wants junk food, sex, and money. If you can learn mission, you'll sell 10 times what people want but don't need or finally sell what no one wants but everyone needs.

A CO-MISSION EXAMPLE

Look what happens when you set up an event for another organization. It serves them unbelievably well. If you hold a high-value program for another outside service that is also looking for business and retention like everyone else, here is what you are providing for them:

1. Their members will be there. Adding value to existing members is the first step to reducing attrition (which we'll be discussing in a later chapter).

2. Your members will show up per your invitation.

3. Your members' referrals will be there.

4. There member's referrels will be there.

For you, this puts you in front of a group of people where 75 percent have not heard your message, are not currently buying your products, or using your services. The great part is, it does the same for your community partner. This is a no-brainer for them. You are coming in, doing the heavy lifting, and putting a group together where three-quarters are potential new customers. Additionally, if you've been community-minded to the degree we have discussed, you can also add value to other partners and utilize the event to highlight one of the charities you serve.

TRANS-MISSION = Win4

Co-mission marketing, as in the example with the gym, creates a win-win-win—win (win^4). The gym, my practice, and the people we each serve benefit. Moreover, when we co-mission we also *trans-mission*. There is a fourth win because we are better when we are together. By pooling our resources and co-missioning we transcend the work we can do on our own. Together, when we trans-mission, we reach more and add greater value to the purpose we share in helping our community.

If you are struggling to build your business or in fear of starting one because you do not know how to market,

I understand. I was reticent to walk into that first gym or restaurant and then got chased out just like I imagined in my worst nightmares. Yet, when I walk in with the intention of starting a relationship with people and organizations I respect, looking for ways to serve them, it is a far easier call to make.

MILLION-DOLLAR BUSINESS AND MILLION-DOLLAR LIFE

Rather than market, create a life. By connecting with the people in your town that you want to work with, you aren't just getting new business and making money, you're creating the life you want.

I wanted to work with charities, coaches, gyms, churches, schools, school boards, first responders, martial arts studios, gymnastics centers, dance studios, health food stores, major businesses, government officials, and professional and elite amateur teams.

In general, the success of any entrepreneurial endeavor is tied to the relationship the leader of that endeavor has with the other leaders in the community. In meeting with leaders of these desirable industries, I discovered the magic of repetition. As you continue to meet people four, five, six times, something supernatural starts to occur. It goes from a distant, cold, or suspicious connection to friendly or even friendship.

When you co-mission, you add value to each other's mission, the organizations receive more benefit than they ever could have on their own, and together you have a far greater impact on the community and the world. The net result is you go beyond your personal missions so that you *trans-mission*.

MISSION + MISSION = TRANS-MISSION.

My partners or co-missioners became those I involved in nearly every component of my education and outreach calendar. They also became some of my closest friends and allies in my work to transform our town from death to life.

The formula looks like this:

Repetition = Relationship

Repetition + Relationship = Partnership

Repetition + Partnership = Co-mission

Co-mission = Transmission

Here's how the process of co-mission to trans-mission works:

1. When you meet someone in the community, the plan is not to get something from them or out of them. The hope is to create a relationship and do life together. To co-mission.

2. Recognize and appreciate the owner, pastor, manager, health care provider, etc. Find sincere reasons you're impressed by what they do and acknowledge their impact and importance in the community. You have an obligation to support them due to the good work that they do.

3. Commit yourself to serving them and helping them achieve their great purpose.

4. Commit yourself to working with them to make a difference in changing this community

5. Ask how they feel you can help.

6. Discuss the action steps you've determined you can take to help THEM. Like my interaction with the Hulk, there should be nothing to say "No" to as you're not asking for anything. You're giving.

7. Trust that, generally, the conversation will turn towards your work. When it does, share your burden for the lives in the community or their organization who need help or are not doing well. You can share specifics as to what you can do to help meet the need and heal the hurt.

GIVE THEM A BIGGER VISION THAN THEY HAVE FOR THEMSELVES

I have spoken to school administrators, dentists, large employers, mechanics, and even pastors who did not have a very large vision for their work. Many people are locked into their box and perceive a low ceiling. I help them see the impact they have on transforming the lives of people in the community and how their work is world-changing.

My friend Dr. James Davis, author of *Making your Net Work* and founder of the Billion Soul Initiative, says, "Those who are not networking soon won't be working." There is one fact evident in the success of the local businesswoman or man; the greater the relationship the leader of a business has with the leaders of other businesses, the more potential for success. Networking is ultimately relationship marketing, which works best when it's not marketing–it is saving lives outside through co-missioning.

It is a crowded marketplace out there. Put an ad in the paper or online and it's getting harder and harder for even you to find it, never mind seeing actual new opportunities coming from it. On the ground (mail), in the air (television/radio), or online (social media/email/website) can get expensive and be difficult topography to navigate when trying to grow and expand. On the other hand, relationships are free and when you have successfully co-missioned, you build networks that make any promotion you invest in more fertile with the possibility of exponential growth.

A FEW EXAMPLES OF CO-MISSION MARKETING

I was a personal trainer in college before the term "personal trainer" was used. Back then you were just the guy or girl at the gym who you could pay to help you work out. Without knowing it, I co-missioned to create a waiting list for my services.

I love wrestling–real wrestling, not pro wrestling. With the knowledge I had attained in nutrition and fitness, I had a passion for giving back to local junior high and high school wrestling programs. For free, I traveled to the different schools in my area and helped the coaches and kids get healthy, make weight, and prep for competition. As a side effect, many of the parents wanted to see the kind of results their kids were seeing and became my clients. They got abs, told their friends about it, and soon I had a thriving guy-who-helps-you-work-out business.

TAKE YOUR TOWN

If you are doing good work, good at what you do, and have something to offer that people truly require in order to thrive, then you need a strategy to take over your region of the world. As you go about co-missioning, what are your best organizations and who are the people with whom it makes the most sense to network? All you commission with are valuable and can ultimately lead to the win.[4] Yet, certain persons, places, or things are more a direct hit for the mission. For example, if your goal is to reach families, churches and schools are loaded with families. If your goal is employees, relationships with HR representatives and CEOs are important. If it is the fitness community, then online health and wellness blog writers, gyms, nutrition stores, and naturally oriented health care providers are all important groups to meet.

THE LITTLE KISSIMMEE MIRACLE

As I spent time going throughout my town, I met with some amazing leaders in the not-for-profit world. With my passion for transformation, I was particularly drawn towards shelters designed to educated, train, and restore people's lives. Living near Walt Disney World Resort, I also found charities that brought families in need into Orlando to bless their lives because they had a sick child or did not have the means to make a trip to the greatest family entertainment location on earth.

My career and essentially my life was launched with the opening of my business in Kissimmee. I began it by working with or for organizations like Give Kids The World, Make-A-Wish, The Dream Center, 4-C Head Start Program, D.A.R.E., the Orlando Union Rescue Mission, the Osceola County Children's Home, and the Coalition for the Homeless. Working with them and many churches and ministries has provided the greatest satisfaction of my life. What I discovered was that in co-missioning, I got to do even more good work than by simply showing up as Dr. Ben Lerner, or one of my company's names, but really looking at how we could serve our local residents or even the world by aligning our co-plans, co-programs, and co-events with one or more of these worthwhile causes. It takes the fun, the effectiveness, the impact, and the relationship to a whole other level. You can add a zero to a relationship, too, when you are giving back to the universe this way.

I call it the Little Kissimmee Miracle. Although now I've shown many people how to do this in many, many different industries. Yet, at the time, the results were unprecedented. I had been co-missioning with a local gym, a powerhouse branded gym, three high schools, and representing multiple charities. We were doing good together, including being in the paper twice for how much food, clothing, furniture, and non-perishable goods we had raised. I had given so much of my time helping the school system, a local Target, and a local Walmart that they all considered me to be part of their staff. The "miracle" was the ringing phone. In a business like mine at the time, it would be normal and a solid start for 30-40 new people to come in during the first 90 days. We had that many on the first day open and in total had nearly 500 new people come in the door during just those first three months. And it didn't stop–over the next three years we had to expand to three more locations in neighboring communities to keep up with that avalanche of growth. All of those locations went from zero to a million. Additionally, the Little Kissimmee Miracle expanded into multiple new businesses that also had million or multi-million start-up trajectories.

GETTING INTO THE NBA

At 5 ft. 6 in. and a 50 percent free throw shooter on a good day, I didn't have much of a chance at making it into the NBA as a player. But being in Orlando, I did want to get in with their NBA team, the Magic. In the nineties, the only professional game in town was the Magic. With Shaq and Penny (Shaquile O'Neal and Anfernee Hardaway) taking the team to the NBA Championship, they were hot. (This is no longer true, but stay with me on this trip down memory lane.)

Because of the Magic influence, I wanted to work with the team. However, this appeared impossible. Professional sports teams require enormous investments by any outside business or vendor that wants to create a relationship with them or be even associated with their name. On the other hand, I believed in the power of mission. In 2000, the Magic traded for who at the time was the heir apparent to Michael Jordan: Grant Hill. A member of the 1996 Olympic Team, Grant was famous for throwing a pass the length of the floor to Christian Laettner with 2.1 seconds left in the round of eight of the NCAA Tournament. Laettner made the basket, or what is now called "The Shot," to allow Duke to beat Kentucky 103-102 and make it to the final four.

Grant Hill coming to Orlando was big news and he was hopefully going to be our new Shaq. Sadly, upon being traded to the Magic, he got injured and could not play. With enough feelers out, I found a friend of a friend who knew Grant. I told her that I would agree to drive to Grant's house to help him every week until we could put him back on the floor. Grant agreed and I worked with him for a couple of years.

An enormous part of mission-based work is your constituents joining your mission. At the time, Grant was a spokesperson for Sprite and McDonald's. I said, "Grant, I realize these are lucrative endorsement deals and I am not judging. But, wouldn't it be great to help save lives instead of promoting just junk food and sugar water?" He smiled and agreed to help me take care of the Orlando Magic. Soon, I was in a meeting with the coach at the time, Doc Rivers, and he agreed to make me a team doctor. Mission works!

CREATING AN ONLINE REVOLUTION!

As we wrap up external promotion and engagement and move to internal promotion and engagement, social media and Internet marketing is a perfect transition. Online needs to work well for both. When it comes to the Internet I like to say, "I paid for Harvard–four times." Early ignorance really caused some damage and cost me a ton of money–or, really, two tons.

Entrepreneurs do not need to be experts in IT or the working on the web, but you do need to know enough to lead others. If anything computer- or smartphone-related seems like absolute witchcraft to you and you are amazed, dazed, and confused by those who appear to have skills or wisdom in these areas, then you can end up in Siberia. I have lost, without exaggerating even slightly, millions of dollars in this arena and fallen behind the industries involved because it all seemed like a miracle to me, and so I just trusted the magic vendors who promised me the moon.

I have learned that I am not alone. Seemingly every entrepreneur, large business owner, pastor, or bowling alley has gotten stung in this fast-paced world of technology and virtual promotion. This short section is not designed to give you the necessary education required to get 700,000 faithful email or Facebook followers, but to create some guidelines and expectations for getting help and moving forward with this important part of your mission.

HERE'S WHERE THEY GET YOU

Where the web experts have killed me and many others is based on a substantive misunderstanding of a valuable outcome based on the speed of the change at which technology moves. I have been charged $50,000 a month for the privilege, pleasure, and promise of having a fancy website, connected to social media and a guaranteed 100,000 Facebook followers. It does sound wonderful and, in fact, the promise was fulfilled–it just wasn't such a privilege or pleasure. Hundreds of thousands of dollars later, I had a stagnant site, with unengaged followers who did not open emails, and no one ever purchased anything or visited one of our centers.

In the torch-a-half-million-dollars example above, we call this the Fantasy Approach. It is this: the vendor will make all of your Internet fantasies come true—the big, beautiful website; a blog; social media pages; an ecommerce platform; even a rotating banner. It seems impossible—you have no idea how it is done, and you do not know who to trust, so you bite the bullet and pay the big bucks. It comes in late, over budget, and not quite what you expected–but that's just the beginning of the problem. In the end, the real issue is that it continues to take work, maintenance, knowledge, content, and there is no return on the investment (ROI).

If the Fantasy Approach has been your experience, I feel your pain. If not, hopefully my pain helps you avoid suffering a similar fate in the future, and I will feel better that my testimony has been a blessing to others.

THE EVOLUTION AND REVOLUTION OF ONLINE SUPPORT

Thankfully, the art of web building and design, along with social media and other forms of online marketing, has become commoditized. With study and effort, almost anyone can do it. As a result, the outcomes you can expect and the cost you should pay are much, much different than the Fantasy Approach. The only way to engage online now—and millions of vendors will want me killed for saying this—is a ROI approach. Do not spend a penny unless it is clear how several pennies are coming back to you. What needs to be done to support your business is no longer voodoo, it is merely an investment that many people can help you with if you know how to guide them and, like any investment, it needs to create a multiple return.

As an example, after dropping the $50,000-a-month guy, I worked with someone who could set up a splash page for under $100. The splash page is almost like a one-page website. We then spent money on some inexpensive, well-targeted

Facebook ads to get people to this splash page. The splash pages we've used have been to sign people up for events, sell products, or bring them into a gym or clinic as a member or for care. For less than $200 on our first project, we got 23 people to an event and 17 signed up for a service that cost more than $2,000. The ROI on $200 was $34,000. Even if it was $800-1,000, or a four- or five-time return, it would have been great—particularly when I had just spent $500,000 for a zero return. What does that negative ROI come out to

THE ROI APPROACH PROCESS

Having a process and experts to help will cost more than a few hundred dollars, but if the machine keeps spitting out a multiple and the ROI is there, then you are following the ROI approach. Again, I am only providing you basics and while I lost enough money on on-line vendors to go to Harvard four times, I still use experts just as I recommend you do. Here is the flow of a solid ROI system.

Step 1: Build Your List and Followers

1. Unless you stumble on some viral miracle, you need to create the necessary lead magnets required to build followers on email and social media. Lists do not grow themselves, so you need incredibly valuable information to give away so that people are willing to part with their email address or honor you with a "Like" or follow request.

2. This is done organically and through paid promotion. Organically, the quality of the information is impressive enough for others to share and pass along. The

paid process helps you either way by getting more eyeballs on whatever magnets you're providing.

Step 2: Keep Giving Them Invaluable Content

1. I'm not going to come to you, buy from you, keep opening up your emails, or following your posts unless I am impressed or entertained, and ultimately trust you. The ROI will be minimal to non-existent if you keep buying ads and promoting your wares without engagement and trust from Step 1 lists and followers. Again, this can be done both organically and paid.

2. The lead nurturing process is taking people at the point they enter your system and providing meaningful content designed to move them along in the understanding, valuing, and trusting of your brand. It should eventually trigger a point where a phone call or direct email reaches out to them at the right time and place for "the sale."

Step 3: Guard Your Reputation

Online reputation through directories like Yelp, Yellow Pages, and Google need to be managed and monitored. These are an important part of your ranking online and a bad reputation can cause friction in your mission.

Step 4: Promotion

1. Now that you have a healthy, engaged, trusting group of people, when you do promotions that cost money and/or time, free and paid promotions will reach more fertile ground.

2. Promote and engage internally and externally. When most people think of promotion, they think of new business. However, communicating and promoting to your existing golden clients improves their engagement and reduces attrition, and they are the most likely to buy or buy-in.

This is no fantasy, so insist on reality and ROI. A steady rhythm of steps 1-4 above should see a continual flow of return while building followers and existing member engagement. Any good local or online vendor should be able to help, at a fair price, and guarantee your return.

chapter 4

SAVING LIVES INSIDE: BUILDING A MISSION-BASED CULTURE

A GAIN, RATHER THAN using language like "internal sales" or "inside marketing and promotion," I call it "Saving lives inside." In a mission-based business, that's the focus, the vision, and the result.

Nothing beats a referral! There is no cost of acquisition, the person comes with trust, they are partially sold on you before coming to your door, website, or phone, they are the most likely to engage, and the most probable with whom to get results. There are only two ways to go about the referral-based business:

1. Coercion and promotion.

2. An organic, mission-based approach.

We all know what coercion and promotion looks like. The first product I manufactured was a more pleasing and palatable version of greens you put in your water to improve its flavor, create a more optimum body pH, and give your beverage some super-beneficial nutrient content. Our first layer of customers bought it and told us they liked everything about it. They liked the taste and thought the price was fair, and it was a really simple product to use. The problem was they didn't tell anyone else about it and we ended up throwing half of the first product run away. Even though my other core businesses by that point had become ultra mission-based, we had taken a very non-mission based approach to the product and requests to tell others. We were constantly trying to convince people to tell their friends or share a coupon, and running promotions designed for them to pass on–which they rarely did. Any promotion is better than none, however it felt more like we had taken a zero away than like we were adding one.

After figuring out our mistake, we were able to build a large product line that has sold over $100 million based on saving lives and not personal product preference alone.

SHIFTING TO A MISSION-BASED CULTURE: GOING ORGANIC

If people are not telling others you are going to be unhappy in whatever work, product, or work product you are providing. There is and incongruence to someone who keeps it to themselves that will slowly suck the soul right out of your body. Plus, no one likes selling and convincing the people who already work with you. It's uncomfortable; it feels like you're being pushy, and the perception–real or imagined–is that you are attempting to use them to make you more money. Like with food, an inorganic referral process is often toxic.

On the other hand, going organic is healthy, enriching, and fulfilling. To get there requires a dynamic shift in the culture. It is an intentional one, but not an impossible one. I've walked into many businesses that could not buy a referral, literally. They offer coupons, bicycles, dinners, and stock options and still see little to no return. The problem: their constituents are not on mission.

THE OFFERING PLATE PHENOMENON: THE ORGANIC END IN MIND.

The number one route to referral, retention, and results in any industry is to get your people on your mission. Once people are not only buying from you, but have bought into what you're doing, you can make the organic shift to the mission-based culture of your dreams.

When I first attended church and they passed the offering plate around, I thought it was really strange, uncomfortable, and off-putting. My brain instantly said, "There it is, it's all about the money. I can't believe they're asking for money in the middle of what is supposed to be our time with God!" However, over time I came to learn the scriptures related to tithing and its spiritual value. As my experience with church grew, I also discovered that this is how a church keeps its doors open. If not for tithes and offerings, there's no bulletins, water in the baptismal, PowerPoint, secretary, guitars, or pastor.

Eventually, I expected, understood, and appreciated the offering plate. This offering plate phenomenon is the ultimate goal of saving lives inside. As you internally promote your events, ask for referrals, and encourage client engagement you'll know they've moved towards your mission when they expect it, appreciate it, and understand why they need to participate. When you do an event, eventually you want them to treat it like an offering plate; they plan to hand over referrals and support.

The offering plate doesn't feel like the pastor is being pushy for money. Similarly, in an organically growing business, joining in aiding the mission becomes a natural conversation about how *we* can improve the community, save lives, and change the world *together*.

YOUR MOST IMPORTANT NEW CUSTOMER IS THE ONE YOU ALREADY HAVE!

A pretty well-known fact in the business community is that a retained customer is far more valuable than a new one. One measure of new business is called "cost of acquisition" (COA). Keeping someone as a client is free. On the other hand, brand new business comes at a cost.

Your COA is the price of all your marketing efforts divided by the number of new people in the door. Therefore, reducing attrition and increasing engagement of existing clientele is enormously valuable. Engagement takes this to another level. Not only is there zero COA, but they refer, they buy, and when on a mission they provide you with new opportunities.

YOUR MOST IMPORTANT CLOSE

The tendency with talks, emails, snail mail, and one-to-one communication with the members and potential new members of your organization is to end up focusing on closing. For current members, you are trying to get them to buy the next product or service. For non-members, you are trying to close them to become a current member. These conversations have value, but not as much value as turning your current members into what we'll call "Warriors."

Warriors are more fully engaged, telling others, and bringing new opportunities to the fore. This is measurable. If you look at particular client, some are 20s, some are 50s, some are 75s, and some are 90s out of 100–where 100 percent is the fully-engaged, on-mission Warrior. So the most important communication, for example, is moving the 20 to a 50 or the 75 to a 90. The most important close is the Warrior close.

Warriors are organic and fun. You want to love going to work on a Monday morning or be happy to be there on your Birthday as well as provide lasting value to people. Warriors are the family you want to spend your week with, who have also co-missioned with you to change the world.

MOVING FROM CUSTOMER TO WARRIOR

Mission Statement: You're Now Entering the Mission Field

If I stood in the entrance of your business or emailed all of your clientele and asked them to recite your mission, could they? How about your staff, could they? "Mission statement" sounds like a trite idea from the eighties, but without vision, people perish. There's not commitment or focus unless the assignment is clear. The larger part of being a Warrior patient or paid member of your team is a clear mission they know so well they can recite it. It's not just knowing, it's also doing. They should know very specifically how they can participate in the fulfillment of the mission.

We put signs up when people leave our businesses that say, "You are now entering the mission field." Yet, you can't just have the sign, you have to also have the understanding. By posting our mission on everything and everywhere and discussing it regularly, we can point to the sign and remind people of how important the mission is.

There are many books out there that discuss how to put together a compelling mission statement. It doesn't have to be overly complicated, but it does have to be bold and encompass reaching the greater part of humanity. Jesus's mission statement to His apostles was, "Make disciples of ALL nations." When they entered the mission field it was clear: go get them all!

A group bigger than them with a purpose greater than theirs

Ideally, you can link what you're doing to make a difference to the same or similar work happening around the globe. The more globally you can position your work, the bigger the impact on the local. People want to see that their little, local participation is making a global difference. When you look at the parabolic success of humanitarian-minded organizations like TOMS Shoes or environmentally-conscious companies like Patagonia, an investment in them is an investment in the planet and its inhabitants. The bigger purpose ten-times your engagement and accelerates your success.

More mission, more results

Experts have found that customers, patients, and members that are on your mission get better results, stay more engaged, and stay. Therefore, the prime objective of any business is to measure customer mission-level on a regular basis.

Winning cultures win and losers lose

When you look at dynasties in sports, you see programs that year after year are in the hunt for the playoffs, Super Bowl, World Series, the Big Dance, or the National Championships, and turn out elite amateur and professional athletes on a consistent basis. These programs have winning cultures. Leaders, administration, coaches, and athletes have committed to something special. On the other hand, there are teams that no matter how great their players are, they keep losing. In professional sports, the teams with the worst records get the top draft choices. Often, five or ten years after having had the top draft picks year after year, the team still stinks. If I sound bitter, it's because I am. I'm a Cleveland Browns fan. When you get drafted in the early rounds by the Browns, no matter your potential, that is likely the end of your career.

A culture is a living, breathing entity impacting every business. Not to sound too hippie-granola-crunchy, but every company has an atmosphere or an energy we call culture and you have to be intentional about making yours a positive one. Being about a great purpose, giving back, transforming lives, on the cutting edge, and having fun are the different tiles that make up the cultural mosaic.

The walls should tell the story. I know my clinic, gyms, or offices have achieved a winning culture when a new person walks in the door and tells us "You are doing amazing work here!" without us having to say a word. The walls, the images, the posted sayings and mission statement, the music, the happy faces of the other clients, staff satisfaction, the credentials, and the energy together speak for themselves.

You can't spread your vision without a team on mission

A mission-based culture stems from a happy, mission-based staff, or what I always call "Team." An old joke tells of a corporate representative coming in to visit one of the regional plants. After touring the facility with the branch manager, the representative asks, "How many people work here?" To which the manager answers, "About 40 percent."

The scary part is, that number is actually high. A Gallup study reported that employee engagement in the U.S. weighs in at only 30 percent. This impact travels deep into your bottom line. It doesn't just mean that your cashier is running credit cards with a frown or numbers are down for the Christmas party. Active disengagement costs the American economy an estimated $450-550 billion per year, and it certainly provides major drag when attempting to go from zero to a million.

Entrepreneurs and companies of all size suffer from venomous staff. This type of staff member *quits, but stays.* In other words, they hate you, they don't like their job, they are only around because they need the money, they are too lazy to go out and find other employment, and/or they are not fully confident that they could find another employer blind enough to hire them. Employees spewing venom can literally paralyze the nervous system of the organization and shut down vital functions necessary to thrive or even stay alive.

VIP Affairs

Have you identified the ideal client yet, or how to define your Warriors? The best advice I ever received was to make sure that every year of your career, you are building your mission-based, lifetime customers. To accomplish this career-making task, time with and in front of your people is the best way to create the lifetime connection for which you are looking. The more they see your heart, perceive you as purpose-driven, and learn more about the mission, the closer they come to the ultimate ideal.

An Example of VIP events:

The VIP meal: I love this one. You take out four or five couples out to eat that have been tremendous members of your business and include some that may be on the fence. After spending time getting to know them in this intimate setting, you allow time for them to share their stories with each other as to how your mission has impacted their lives.

To check the pulse of my best people and find out how I am doing, I always start with the statement, "I believe you all know that this is my calling or mission and not a business." Their responses both verbal and non-verbal tell the story of how well I've behaved and communicated mission to them.

As dinner or lunch is wrapping up, and I've had some one-on-one time with everyone and they have all had an opportunity to share, we get to work. First, I want to make sure they know this meal was about thanking them and serving them better. I then go into the crisis in our community and how through the work we do with them, they are being saved. We get very specific about how their engagement serves them and get commitments to future products and services designed to take their lives to another level.

Next, I take out a notebook, get very serious, and ask three important questions. The context of these questions continues to revolve around maximizing my service to them and also how we can take this mission to Main Street so we can save even more lives. As with all questions, we are looking to reinforce the great decision they have made to be a member of the movement.

The 3 Questions:

1. What was it that most attracted you to us and made you into such a model part of the mission?

2. What can we do to serve you better?

    2a. Talk them through how you can help them achieve greater success, health, prosperity, etc., through the work you do and actually sign them up for the next opportunities available that you offer to improve their lives.

3. How do we save more lives?

Again, mission participation means better results and less attrition. When this goes well, you will get lengthy and voluminous feedback on strategies to reach the community and end up taking down the names of the many people they want you to call who need your help. All as a part of making the world a better place. Consider VIP dinners, VIP parties, barbecues, workshops, invitation-only entertainment opportunities, and any other events you can think of at which to interact, share testimonies, and ask some version of these questions. This is a game-changer. It will not only take you from Zero to a Million, but will sustain you year upon year. Most entrepreneurs groan when they realize in five to ten years that, in the hustle and bustle of business, they did not create the 25-50 warriors a year they needed. Instead, the tendency is to let engagement take care of itself and let people come and go rather than intentionally building lifetime clients through VIP affairs.

Customer Insight: Are we moving towards or away from Warrior status?

Customer insight has been my capstone to success, particularly in service-based industries. In every interaction, there are a handful of items that you and your team have to utilize your emotional intelligence in to discern and act upon. For example:

1. Does it appear that the customer understands the value of the service?

2. Are they engaged or does it appear they are slipping out the door?

3. Have they participated in recent events or communications important for them to grow as a client?

4. Are they an active member of the mission–referring, making suggestions, and helping to create opportunities for the business?

The best way to encourage these behaviors is not to point out which number needs work or to 'punish" the client. Rewarding and acknowledging the right, mission-based actions is the best way to see those actions continued. You know you're in a good place as an organization when reinforcing good behavior is far outweighing punishing the bad.

Reinforcements like celebrating when someone comes in for their appointments as scheduled, calls to reschedule rather than just missing, or gets results go a very long way. Giving gifts for referrals or reaching milestones is a sure way to see people do it again. I always have my staff "on the lookout!" At the end of the day, I want people on a call list that fall into three categories:

1. Usher in the new. Call people that are right at the beginning of the journey or have just received their initial product or service. In so many cases, their mind is blown that you called. This leaves a positive, indelible mark!

2. There are issues. There is nothing better than a call from the owner when it comes to re-routing a customer that has gotten off track or is having a problem with your company. On thousands of occasions, maybe tens of thousands, my staff has thought a client had reached a point of no return only to have me give them call, have them deeply appreciate it, and get right back on track.

3. To acknowledge. These I love: Making a call to acknowledge anyone that did anything at all that is good for the mission and needs to be thanked.

4. This call list makes the 20- to 30-minute drive home from the office one of the most productive times of your career, and the future of your mission-based business.

COMMUNICATING YOUR MESSAGE OUTSIDE AND INSIDE OF YOUR BUSINESS

Learning the Elaboration-Likelihood Model

The Elaboration-likelihood Model (ELM) references the fact that when you attempt to share your messaging, marketing, and ideas with the public, there are two types of audiences you must consider:

1. People who are moved by superficial information and fail to evaluate the content.

2. People who are truly mindful of the message and consider the details.

Educational messages delivered in person, on a website, in books, brochures, or through social media are most impactful when the producer knows if those in receipt of the information are going to superficially and unconsciously consider it or take a captive, focused approach. The concept of ELM contains both Peripheral and Central audience types.

1. **Peripheral Type:** The peripheral audience is focused on the periphery; the superficial, easy-to-process data and the features of a message rather than its deeper meaning. In this case, they are primarily on auto pilot and really not thinking through it. Consequently, they may just take the data at face value simply because the source is considered an expert, is well known, or is a trusted leader in the space. Peripherally focused individuals rely on cues that tip to popularity, like how many followers, views, or likes on social media

something has, or the conventional acceptability of the information because it is the way it has always been done, rather than giving it much thought.

2. **Central Type.** The central audience are those that intentionally think through and evaluate message content. They do not make a quick, gut, or blink decision but rather utilize their training and experiences to determine whether or not the persuasive message is compelling and whether or not they should change their perspective as a result.

This issue is incredibly relevant in promotion and persuasive messaging. It is mission-critical that promoters determine whether or not those they are attempting to reach are apt to make a decision based simply on rules of thumb or if they are going to thoughtfully comb through the information in an effort to learn and draw a logical, well thought-out conclusion.

How mission based organizations like Susan G. Komen and the pink campaign use ELM, central and peripheral routes, to gain massive conversion.

The pink campaign has gained enormous attention and momentum over the previous decades, above and beyond other very similar promotions. Nearly every major industry, celebrity, and politician goes pink in October. This includes the products that cause cancer, like cookies and fried food. Therefore, the Komen promotional model, regardless of what you think about the movement itself, has been studied very carefully.

In assessing ELM and the Susan G. Komen campaign to fight breast cancer, they clearly make efforts to talk to both the central and peripheral audiences.

They reach the peripheral people perhaps better than any pitch in history. Utilizing messaging that revolves around the pink, the color alone now influences people to trust in their brand and support it. Their website and materials utilize very high-level facts and figures that do not necessarily hold up or tell the whole story. As an example, the costs related to cancer are projected to increase dramatically in the future, but Komen statistics say otherwise. If closely investigated, it is easy to see that gains in this area of health are slim, but on the surface they provide a version of the data necessary for their target audience to believe that supporting organizations like theirs is working to eliminate the disease in the future.

In today's social media, *People* magazine, reality television star, click-bait society, where the Komen example of ELM really shines is in the use of corporate and celebrity partnering. The entire month of October is pink month and sports teams, corporations, and shopping malls turn their clothing, accessories, and materials pink to represent this brand. To build peripheral credibility, their website features corporate partners like Ford, New Balance, American Airlines, the NCAA, and the NFL. Celebrities like Bob Saget, Julianne Moore, Ellen DeGeneres, James Woods, George W. Bush, and Trisha Yearwood all associate themselves with the campaigns, further encouraging the public to simply take any messaging at face value.

For their central people, they employ multiple components related to learning the intricacies of breast cancer and all of the overall related issues. The detail begins with resources that outline anatomy and continues to trace steps throughout the maturation process of breast development from puberty through menopause. Specifics related benign and malignant breast cancer and how to know the difference are offered in a very centralized, detailed manner. They fall under headings like "Warning signs," "Did you know," and "Survival rates," in order to give people the full weight of the statistics being shared.

The biology, stats, statistics, and related scare tactics are tremendously effective for those motivated by central concepts and give depth to the campaign.

HOW THIS WORKS FOR YOU:

1. Peripheral: use this type of superficial, celebrity or expert endorsed branding in your blogs, social media posts, pamphlets, videos, or anything else that will appeal to an audience just looking for a quick read or view.

    It has been found in community funding campaigns that business owners respond better to hyperbole and the success the organization is having in raising funds than to actual facts and data. The power of corporate and celebrity endorsement and the overstating of the impact a particular group is having has become an actual cause of concern.

2. Central: For people that are analytical and experienced in their field, they will want data. For example, because I am in health care, I am least swayed by the peripheral route. While expert endorsement can influence me in areas of finances, spirituality, relationships, and personal growth, I have been studying, researching, teaching, and writing in the areas of anatomy and

physiology, health care, and lifestyle for 25 years. As a result, I deeply analyze the content and it needs to be scientific, well researched, and proven in a clinical setting for me to become influenced. The only peripheral cue I will respond to is whether or not the information comes from a credible source.

A celebrity or corporate endorsement would have the opposite impact on me as I am looking for experts with a higher level of scientific background and would be suspicious as to what steps were skipped or where money was invested improperly in bringing in that type of corporate branding. There is research that has shown that when it comes to health care in particular, the quality of the information and the credibility of the source has the most influence on recipients.

BINGE ON THIS, NOURISH WITH THAT

Understanding what qualifies as peripheral, or central, and when to use it.

Peripheral: In essence, this is social proof. Like 200 likes on a Facebook post, the post has been proven scientifically to have greater acceptance as does anything that appears popular and accepted, or provides goodwill to the community or, better yet, the world, and is affiliated with celebrities or the well-known. It is also the information that discloses the extremes of consequence, good or bad, to someone's choices, decisions, or indecision. The more quotes from experts and actual celebrities, or perceived credible endorsements and testimonies you can get, the more powerful the peripheral impact. For example, my work with Olympic and professional sports goes further online, in a bio, or in an introduction, than the fact that I have three degrees and provide a proven, scientific approach to my products and services.

Central: This is the actual science, data, process, or functionality of chiropractic, the nervous system, research on lifestyle and adjustments, lengthy education, longer blogs, videos, and articles. It is the legitimate information providing real proof versus social proof that something is viable and effective.

Central celebrity endorsement: Celebrities, your celebrity status, the work of your foundation, the work you do with sports, the strength of any goodwill initiative you are a part of, any important community programs, political connections, etc. are vital to your Komen-like approach. While you may not know Oprah, President Obama, President Trump, or Lebron James, any affiliations are a leg up.

Here's the key to use: Peripheral *moves* and Central *keeps*.

Peripheral moves: If you're attempting to create movement, binge on peripheral when creating—conversions, likes on Facebook, downloads, shares, purchases. It is also important in brief, passing situations like the short visit a customer makes to your place of business, social media, a blog, or email; you must focus on peripheral or make peripheral a substantive part of the material. A portion of the population is moved by central, but it's the minority of really smart and inquiring or truly cynical people that are out there.

Central keeps: Nourish people with data over time and when there are longer periods of time, like with a talk, a video, a piece of literature, an email nurture campaign, or a book, etc.

It's the combination of both at the right time, and providing them both all of the time, that works to not only convert people to the mission, but keeps them there. Potential and current customers who get a heavy dose of both consistently and at the right time start and they stay. If your corporate colors are turquoise or lavender, the goal is a turquoise or lavender world, and ELM can take you there.

Chapter **5**

CAPACITY: A PRODUCT OF STRUCTURE AND FLOW

YOU ARE THE LEVEL of your business. What do I mean by that? Having been involved in ownership or management of gyms, chiropractic clinics, and dental offices in particular, it has become clear to me that each of these has a "capacity." Capacity works by placing a ceiling on the amount of people you can see or manage in a given day, week, or month. Once you hit that number, roadblocks inherent in the structure, function, and flow of your business halt any more growth. These road blocks are also called "capacity blocks." This is seen when a business invests time and dollars into marketing, funneling in a number of new customers in a particular month much greater than the norm. Yet, within a short period of time, despite the influx of more people, overall production ends up the same. In fact, because of the additional stress on the system, sometimes the numbers even end up lower as parts and people breakdown.

However you measure your success, you are the number you are at or stuck at.

1. If you are a salon that serves 17 people per day and you can't get past 17 people per day, you know why? You're a 17-people-a-day salon.

2. If you keep netting $8,000 a month no matter what you try in your business, you know why? You are an $8,000-a-month business.

3. If you are a dentist and, regardless of the new technology you add, increased marketing budget, or employee training, you see 50 patients per week, you know why? You're a 50-patients-per-week dentist–that's why.

On the other hand, others have raised the roof. Their capacity is 100s of people per day and scalable to an unlimited number—millions of dollars per month, or thousands of clients per week. Virtually every entrepreneurial endeavor has some capacity, but if that ceiling is lower than you desire, then you likely need to address structure, function, and flow.

STRUCTURE

Don't practice until you get it right, practice until you can't get it wrong. —Nick Saban, National Championship Winning Football coach.

Structure is the combination of process and execution. If the processes aren't effective and scalable, you don't have the right people, or the training has been inadequate, then the bones of the operation are faulty and unstable.

Every business and all of the units within should have a playbook that outlines the steps and scripts. The best companies and teams in the world with the highest employee satisfaction have a very specific manual–a playbook. It allows for people and divisions to train like they are preparing for the Super Bowl. This includes live training on how to manage real-life challenges, objections, and situations that occur regularly so you are ready.

I wrestled for 20 years. It was always fun when someone who never wrestled before would want to take me on. These newbies would try to take me down without fully grasping the fact that I had trained tens of thousands of times on how to defend the lame move they were trying for the first time. I could see their meager effort coming from a mile away, smile, and hurt them. Your teams should be over-trained on dealing with every scenario so that when a challenge arises, you can smile, execute, and win-win.

Without structure, you cannot manage. If you are making a product like a professional tennis racket and it's being produced in an assembly line, it is easy to manage your success and correct your failure. If at the end of the line, the racket is missing strings, troubleshooting is easy. You know to go to stage four of the assembly, where the strings are strung, and correct the malfunction. If you do not have a playbook with steps or processes designed to take a product or customer from point A to point G, how can you determine where you need work?

For example, in our chiropractic, nutrition, or dental clinics we have a three-day process. There is an evaluation on day one, a review of findings and start of protocol on day two, and a care plan on day three. If something breaks down, it is like the tennis racket: I can go right to the stages down the line and see where we are malfunctioning. If people are not getting started with care or not seeing positive results, we are able to go back and check. Which day is it? Are the team members following the playbook on that day? This allows us to check each step of the process, assess whether we're executing by the book, and if we are performing well to assess the feedback to see where our processes need to improve.

THE FLOW

Flow is the invisible capacity blocker. Imagine you are running a busy kitchen like you see on one of those behind-the-scenes restaurant cooking shows. Your kitchen has all of the latest technology, appliances, cutlery, pots and pans, and cooking experts necessary to delivery the finest quality cuisine. There is only one challenge: the refrigerators are in the basement, the pots and pans are in the bathroom, the non-perishable foods are outside in storage, the cutlery is upstairs, and...you get the picture. You can have the best materials, equipment, and team members, but if it's not in an orderly flow, you won't function no matter how good your playbook is.

I built one of the largest clinics of any kind in the world. As we made the climb from Zero to a Million and then millions, flow was the consistent challenge. At one point, we were busting at the seams seeing 600 people each week, but once we learned how to maximize flow, we were seeing over 2,000 people each week—and often seemed slow. Something as simple as patients knowing how to move themselves from the front door to the treatment rooms increased our capacity by hundreds of people each day.

They say "Technology only enables process–it doesn't create process." By finding software that allowed people to check themselves in, that caused their records to pop up when they entered a patient care room, and had all of the information visible for the doctor to properly treat them, we increased our capacity by hundreds again.

Additionally, by properly delegating tasks that did not require a licensed health care provider away from them and to well-trained team members, we could remove choke points to patient flow and, again, blow right through our capacity ceiling. A Harvard study showed that health care facilities that see the most people provided the highest quality of care and service. It sounds counter-intuitive unless you understand flow. By removing capacity blocks and allowing specialized personnel to focus on the work they've been trained to do, you do more volume more effectively.

Our vision has always been that people would drive by dozens of similar businesses or scroll down the page on Google past others who offer the same service who are cheaper and more convenient than us. Why would they? Because we're more competent, we execute better, and we love them and care more about our community. So they make the trip to get us!

THE TRANSITION

The promises of God do not come without the processes of God.

Most of us live in transition. Our lives are in transition, our country is in transition, our family is in transition, our company is in transition, and we are in a personal growth transition. Transition is where one door is closing and another is opening. However, if you don't move quickly and effectively to the other door, that one may close too. In between any door is a hallway–though many pastors like to take out the first "a" and replace it with an "e."

To get through this *hellway* successfully—particularly if you feel you already know the preponderance of wisdom there is to know in the world—you have to realize that breakthroughs aren't discovered with warehouses full of new knowledge, some new device, or a radical breakthrough in the day one process or a new IPO coming onto the stock market. Tearing down strongholds that stunt your growth at any level comes from smaller and smaller insights that put cracks in the ceiling that allow breakthrough.

Ignorance is not bliss. What you don't know is killing you. Hosea 4:6 doesn't say, "My people are blissful for lack of knowledge." It says, "My people perish for lack of knowledge." To break through and save more lives–including your own—you need the facts!

As I went from locally competitive to nationally and then college-ranked in wrestling, I racked up thousands of hours of practice. As a result, practices, off-season camps, and special trainings stopped being about learning the next huge move. Instead, any ability to get better and beat elite competition came from literally learning small things. For example, I'd learn that my thumb had to go in front of the bicep and not behind on my high crotch defense, or to shift my right hip out two inches before standing up when the opponent lined up on my left side. It wasn't learning Russian pretzel holds or the Iranian skull crusher that took you from also-ran to the podium, but removing blind spots, improving technique, and being reminded of the small stuff that made all the difference. Who are your coaches? Who are your mentors? Where are your examples of greater success? Where are you getting the facts necessary that allow you to fine-tune your approach and get better?

After the facts cause the cracks in your ceiling capacity, the power to break through is focus. The clients I have worked with who struggle the most over the years are the ones who struggle to keep their eye on the prize and focus on the next, most important task until complete. We will leave a meeting in agreement of the next step, but when we reconvene and I ask them the results of that action, they bring me the next problem. Problems have a cause, and focusing on the core causes rather than jumping to the next effect that pops up never got anyone anywhere.

Have you seen the *Karate Kid* movies? I am probably dating myself, but if you haven't seen at least the first one, then you have an assignment to see it. It is necessary viewing. If you want to see more than the first one, keep watching until either Pat Morita is no longer Miyagi or Ralph Macchio is no longer Daniel.

In the first movie, when Daniel bows to honor Mr. Miyagi, he looks down. Miyagi smacks him and says, "Daniel-San, look eye. Always look eye." He's reinforcing a cardinal rule of battle and in life: Don't take your eyes off the enemy in a fight. Similarly, don't take your eyes off of your assignment or be distracted by what's crawling around you in life, either.

If you struggle, it is rarely that you're not powerful enough. You carry the Light of the world and you are called to be light.

If you consider the properties and impact of light, the basic lightbulb does not do much. It merely disperses a little bit of energy just enough to illuminate a small space. However, if you focus that same light you can create a laser powerful enough to blow a hole through a wall. In fact, focus more and the light can actually touch the moon.

In *Walden*, Henry David Thoreau wrote, "The mass of men lead lives of quiet desperation"—to which someone added "and died with their song still inside of them." Thoreau wrote during a time of transition from the agricultural age to the industrial age. As we move from the information age to the over-informed technology age, Rick Warren has added, "People have moved from quiet desperation to aimless distraction." Smartphones, the Internet, and 24/7 availability of 500 television stations have turned our lasers into lanterns. We're barely lighting up a closet, never mind being the light of the world.

When Abraham rescues Lot's family from Sodom and Gomorrah, God tells them to focus on the future and not get distracted by looking around. Lot's wife looks back and turns into a pillar of salt. *Look eye, Lot's wife, look eye.*

Christian folk are told to fix our eyes upon Jesus–the "author and finisher of our faith" (Heb 12:2). It is hard to stay focused as we face the hurdles that lay between our current condition and the promises of God. But realized, the promises of God do not come without the processes of God. Get the help, get the training, and look-eye!

chapter **6**

KEEPING YOUR MIND ON YOUR MONEY AND YOUR MONEY ON YOUR MIND

S TRONG FINANCIAL LEADERS START their morning off with a cup of coffee and today's cash flow analysis. While *People* magazine, ESPN, or your most pressing task sound like a better way to kick off your day, you've got to stay focused on the money if you want to succeed in business.

Millions of dollars are found in tightly managing your cash. Cash flow is called "The lifeblood of the business" and a failure to manage the pennies can choke the life and the joy right out of you and your mission from God. Poor stewardship won't be God's fault and when you pray for God to help, He'll just remind you of the Parable of the Talents (Matt. 25:14-30).

One of my friends and business associates became wealthy running yogurt and snack shops. He sells $3-$5 dollar items, generates solid profits, has grown to three locations, and created the funds to buy some of the real estate. That is called "Good stewardship when the amounts are small." For an entrepreneur, having a yogurt shop approach to the dollars going in and out is what we call a good mindset about money, or being truly cash conscious.

This is not a book to cover every detail and give you all of the resources required to manage your business. But there are enough details, information about stewardship, and resources in this chapter to make you financially very, very happy at home. It certainly did that for me. You do not have to be a 12th degree black-belt accountant to be doing a fine job. But you cannot skip the basics and avoid severe monetary pain and injury. Going from an idea to a profitable, sustainable, and predictable business requires a strong financial hand. People with great vision who fail to make the numbers work is almost a proverb, and it is a parable (Luke 14:28-30). Accounting practices, cash flow analysis, profit and loss (P&L) statements, budgets, EBITDA (Earnings before interest, taxes, depreciation, and amortization), and weekly, monthly, quarterly, and annual goals are mature essentials that are irreducible minimums for long-term prosperity. These terms go down like a rat sandwich to most entrepreneurs, but you need to learn to love them, date them, take them to dinner and a movie, propose to them, and get married.

Even if it's a meeting with just you and you, you and your spouse, or you and your accountant, you need to meet at a minimum weekly to go over money. Any financial analysis reviews:

1. Current bank statement.

2. Cash in the bank.

3. P&L statement by area or department (See Figure X)

4. Assessment of services and products provided

5. Billings against collections.

You should go into this analysis with very specific expectations. If I randomly looked at a business I am unfamiliar with and reviewed the above, I wouldn't know right away if this was standard, improving, or going backwards. You should know your numbers in your sleep—what production you expect, as well as costs and collections as a percent of that production.

As an example:

1. I generally sell 100 yogurts a day for $5 each.

2. The raw cost of the yogurt is supposed to be $1 per serving.

3. My overall cost per transaction (CPT) is $3 (including rent, staff, utilities, leases, insurances, machine maintenance, and materials.).

4. The gross profit is $2 per sale.

That overall expense is tricky. Many new business owners and most of the staff believe the profit is $4/sale. But, you take the total overhead and divide by the number of transactions and you get a cost per transaction—which is the $3 and therefore only $2 in profit per sale. This means if someone steals a yogurt or the owner's family comes in and everyone is eating "free" yogurt, you are losing $3 each time and making it harder and harder to turn a profit.

Weekly yogurt shop financial analysis should be:

1. I sold 500 yogurts Monday-Friday.

2. I collected $2,500 for the week in yogurt sales ($5 x 500).

3. My overall profit and loss shows $2,500 less $1,500 ($3CPT x $500) = $1,000.

So as you look at your weekly financial form, these are the numbers you expect to see, and ultimately you plan on $1,000 a week remaining in your account after expenses come out. As you review these numbers each week, you will often find that something is not adding up. Thankfully, because you are looking, you can investigate the malfunction and address it before you have financial stress or go broke.

IMPORTANT SMALL BUSINESS NUMBERS TO KNOW

1. Total collections divided by total products sold or services provided = Dollars per transaction (DPT).

   Example: If the store collected $15,000 and sold 3000 yogurts, it's a $5 DPT. If a massage therapists clinic collected $15,000 and performed 300 massages, it's a $50 DPT.

   If less than $5 or $50 and those are the fees you are charging, something is off in the business or the data collected.

1. Total overhead divided by total transactions = Cost per transaction (CPT)

   Example: If the yogurt shop has an overhead of $10,000/month and sells 3000 yogurts then it cost them $3.33 per yogurt. If the massage therapist has an overhead of $10,000/month and did 300 massages, then it costs $33.33 per massage.

1. DPT – CPT = Profit per transaction

   Example: $5 per yogurt - $3.33 = $1.67

   $50 massage - $33.33 = $16.67

Figure X shows how you can review this by department and overall in your business each and every week. The weekly financial form is the "holy spreadsheet.

FIGURE X: YOUR WEEKLY FINANCIAL FORM

Services:

Service #1

	Week 1	Week 2	Week 3	Week 4	Week 5	Total
Collections						
Expenses						
Profit						
Total						

Service #2

	Week 1	Week 2	Week 3	Week 4	Week 5	Total
Collections						
Expenses						
Profit						
Profit %						

Billing/Collections

	Week 1	Week 2	Week 3	Week 4	Week 5	Total
Collected						
Billed						
Profit						
Profit %						

Miscellaneous

	Week 1	Week 2	Week 3	Week 4	Week 5	Total
Payroll						
Cash taken by owner						
Supplies taken by owner						
Office supplies						
Total						

Products:

Retail/Wholesale

	Week 1	Week 2	Week 3	Week 4	Week 5	Total
Product #1						
Expenses						
Profit						
Profit %						
Product #2						
Expenses						
Profit						
Profit %						
Product #3						
Expenses						
Profit						
Profit %						
Product #4						
Expenses						
Profit						
Profit %						
Total						
Collected						
Total Expenses						
Total Profit						
Total Profit %						

Total Expenses

	Week 1	Week 2	Week 3	Week 4	Week 5	Total
Total Collections						
Total Expenses						
Profit						
Profit %						

Two quick horror stories to increase your zeal for regularly checking the numbers:

1. In my own practices and businesses, as well as with the many people I have coached, I have learned of holes in billings and collections or issues with inventory control that have been costing hundreds, thousands, or even tens of thousands of dollars each month for many years. In looking back, we often do the math and the amount of money that has been lost could solve world hunger for some, and for others it would've been the difference between no paycheck and something that could be taking care of their family.

2. Theft. One of my earliest clients had been doing very well in his business for years—or at least his office manager had. My client could not figure out how such a thriving practice had such moderate profitability. In starting this weekly financial process we unearthed the reality that his manager, who was his cousin, had stolen over $1 million through a scheme plotted out over several years.

TAKE A BITE OUT OF CRIME

When you are looking at the bank statements–which includes the deposits–every week, looking at cash on hand, regularly reviewing those P&Ls, and managing your QuickBooks or working closely with someone else who is, it gets really hard to steal without being some kind of hacker or criminal mastermind. But if you're not looking, it's not hard to steal a nut from a blind squirrel.

CASH VS. CASH FLOW

Profit and cash flow can be two different things if you are not taking into account payables that do not apply regularly. A monthly P&L, for example, may show that you profited $10,000. Many entrepreneurs look at that as free cash and may spend it on bills or a new Ferrari. What you may miss are those quarterly, annual, or semi-annual taxes, vendor payments, insurance bills, and other items that are not accounted for every month.

Remember, it is cash *flow* that is the lifeblood of every business and not just "cash." I have a dental office I consulted for that considered their billings to be real cash and looked at any money left over at the end of the month as free cash. Then, on a regular basis, the poor dentist kept getting hit with bills, surprises, and the financial realities of maintaining equipment. He would have to pull from holy, untouchable resources like personal savings and personal credit cards to pay the bills. He could not figure out why his net worth was on a downslide despite a fairly successful dental office.

Make sure you either amortize these annual costs into your monthly P&L analysis or look at an accounting of these items alongside that P&L or you'll get the shock of cash versus cash flow. Cash flow is what really remains after every debt, bill, or the price of doing business is paid. Focus in on that number–it's the only real one!

PAY GOD AND YOURSELF

Ideally, you are pulling out 10 percent for the church and 10 percent for your personal future. Assuming you're not one light bill away from going under, pay God and yourself first and figure out the bills from there.

WHAT THE MONEY IS FOR

Warren Buffett, one of the richest men in history, said, "If you're in the luckiest one percent of humanity, you owe it to the rest of humanity to think about the other 99 percent."

The money is for doing good. The common response to Mr. Buffett's sentiment is, "Sure, if I had billions I'd give some away too." Yet, the rich will tell you that it was their giving, servant's heart that made them the money. It was their belief that easing the burden of others is what the money is for that drove them and helped them become a success.

SETTING UP YOUR FINANCIAL BUCKETS!

A common problem when I first started opening up franchises was that my young franchisees could not pay their taxes. They did not realize that fees, lunch money, and dishwashing detergent come from after-tax dollars and not before.

The best and easiest way to manage money is to set up different accounts with different purposes.

There are many ways to do this, but I recommend using five buckets:

1. Operating account

This needs to have the minimum amount necessary to operate your business monthly. Ideally, it actually carries a three- to six-month reserve. Taking all of the money out as personal spending money and hoping for the best when it comes to making payroll the next month is not recommended.

2. Tax account

If you're in the 30 percent tax bracket, then take 30 percent off the top of your profits and get it out of both your hands and your mind. It's not your money, and when the accountant calls on or before April 15, no matter how bad the news is you won't even care the money will be in the account.

3. Personal operating

This is where you transfer your salary and dividend checks for running your life, paying your family's bills, tithing, and to move into your investments.

4. Future business purchases

Buy things you can afford. You know you can afford them when you can pay for them. You don't just buy new technology, a piece of equipment, or software upgrade because you want it or in many cases even need it. You do it when you have the money to do it. Sometimes going into debt to pay

ZERO TO A MILLION IN A YEAR

for tools that have the capacity to increase earnings is worth it. Yet, ideally you use actual money.

If you want to get the new Mac for video editing and it's $2,500, you begin to load up this account from the operating account and earmark it for the new Mac. When the account hits the mark, then you buy it.

5. Future personal purchases

The same rules apply at home. While some personal items and transportation may be utilized through your corporation, through the recommendation of your accountant, most of what you buy for yourself, your family, or your home comes out of personal operating.

You load this bucket from the personal operating account similar to the future business purchase. If you want a trip to Hawaii, a new car, a new couch, or a 60-inch plasma television, you buy it when the money is in the bucket.

6. Investments

You have to commit to a number or percentage that goes into your financial future. This often requires remarkable intestinal fortitude and the impressive ability to resist alluring purchases or family members that do not understand at all why we aren't spending all we're making. One way to protect this investment is to get the process out of your hands. Just like the auto draft that should be set up to pay a utility company, a set amount should leave your account immediately towards debt or investments.

No investment is better than this one.

While there are circumstances where debt can be used as leverage to build an empire, for the typical entrepreneur, and most human beings, debt is prison. When you look at the return on eliminating debt, it is hard to argue the enormous and powerful ROI—interest goes away, overhead goes down, peace of mind goes up, and you can focus on the mission rather than the bills.

KILLER HABITS

Are you in a "health crisis" today, or are you "lifestyling" yourself into a health crisis? Medical bills and lost work days create major financial losses, not to mention what poor health can mean to your way of life or if you'll be alive at all! Not only do these habits lead us towards crisis, the cost on the way there is enormous. A daily Starbucks, eating out, alcohol, cigarettes, a thousand movie channels, useless reading material, costly apps and websites you subscribe to, and so on add up to tens if not hundreds of thousands of dollars over a number of years and distract you and your finances from being put to good use.

Take the Killer Habits Test: List your habits and the cost and see where this adds up:

Cost of the Habits:

Unnecessary Habit #1: _____

Amount saved by quitting:

_____ per week _____ per month

Unnecessary Habit #2: _____

Unnecessary Habit #3: _____

Amount saved by quitting:

_____ per week _____ per month

Total saved if your dropped the Habits:

_____ per week _____ per month

What can you do today to stop your "habit"?

PERSONAL FINANCIAL GOALS

Based on the people I know in similar professions, the training in finances I received by attending seminars and reading books, and what seemed possible to me at the time, I set a very specific set of goals for money after opening up my first business. The goals were to eliminate debt in one year, begin investing a minimum of 20 percent of my collections into a diversified portfolio, and to have $1 million of liquid assets in four years. Because of many of the principles I have shared so far, and even with several personal tragedies and big mistakes along the way, I achieved this goal in three years, while still in my twenties.

Certainly Facebook founders, software prodigies, and dot.com geniuses have become billionaires and not millionaires in their twenties. But those guys and girls are the one-hundreth of one percent. Like many of you reading this book, I came from a long line of "thousandaires." So those extra zeros meant a whole lot to me. I also had chosen a career path where the average income was $70,000 a year, with an average debt burden of about $200,000. Once I accomplished this first goal, I could take a deep breath and work on expanding my vision beyond any limitations of family, peers, and profession about earning potential, and begin to learn and grow.

MORE MONEY TIPS FOR ENTREPRENEURS

1. Setting up an IRA, 401K, or other retirement plan can be a great move, but watch out for costs. Many if not most programs, while saving on taxes, are cost-prohibitive. The right one enables you to stash away a whole lot of money, tax-deferred.

2. Incorporating moves liability and some cost away from you personally. Get with your accountant on how you can legally use pre-tax dollars for expenses.

3. You keep 100 percent of what you don't spend and only a fraction of what you make. I have a friend who owns several small pizza shops. They don't bring in millions, but he keeps more money than many, many businesses that do. It's 900 square feet, a couple of ovens, and large, cheap industrial bags and cans of white flour, mozzarella cheese, and tomato sauce. His overhead is practically in the hundreds of dollars. Every penny you don't spend on sticky notes and paper clips goes to the bottom line. When you make money, some substantive part of the money you bring in is eaten by costs.

4. Don't just have an office budget, have a home budget! You can use software like mint.com, a spreadsheet, or do it old-school by hand. You need to figure out your fixed costs based on items like housing, utilities,

insurances, childcare, and transportation, and create an allotted, capped amount that you track to spend on un-fixed costs like health care, housing, personal expenses, food, clothing, entertainment, and luxuries.

5. Don't leave a hole in the safety net! Make sure you have a good lawyer when signing or putting together agreements. By skipping the attorney, you may save thousands of dollars now, but it can cost you tens of thousands of dollars later – or much more! Make sure you are fully covered with business insurance, liability, and disability. These bills hurt and may never have an ROI, but they protect you from the potential of your mission going down the tubes.

6. Best receivables and payables practices.

   a. Collect receivables ASAP, including offering a discount for early or one-time payments.

   b. Many payables to vendors and suppliers are negotiable. This is particularly important with inventory. If you can push payments out six weeks, to 90 days, it gives you time to breathe as well as turn some of that inventory.

7. Give bonuses and raises from the "up". Create ownership thinking by tying key team members to the bottom line. Like an owner, their finances go up when profits do. If cash is flat and performance is too, then raises based on time in the seat can erode cash flow and put the company in jeopardy. (See more on bonuses in the Team Building section).

FOCUSING ON THE RIGHT THINGS

Winners have simply formed the habit of doing things losers don't like to do. —Albert Gray

As we've covered, finances are a matter of focus. Even modestly successful businesses, when paying attention to the bottom line, can normally generate a profit.

One of the greatest benefits for me in my travels with the U.S. teams was the opportunity to learn more about the winning principles common among the world's top coaches and athletes. At the 2000 Olympic Trials in Dallas, Texas, there was a special event following the competition where Olympic team coach and former Olympic gold medalist Dan Gable spoke. I doubt that any one athlete knows more about winning than he does. Gable was a three-time All-American, a three-time Big Eight champion, a two-time NCAA National Champion, and a gold medalist at the 1972 Olympics. As a coach, he won nine consecutive NCAA Championships (1978–86).

At the event honoring his career, Coach Gable told one story with deep meaning about winning. At the 1972 Olympics in Germany, the U.S. Olympic team had a sure winner: a heavyweight wrestler named Chris Taylor. Chris was the heaviest Olympian ever at 412 lb., before today's 360 lb. limit. He was also a technically sound wrestler. The assumption was that he'd easily win a gold medal because not only was he good, he was just too big for anyone to really be able to wrestle. One of Taylor's competitors was a Greco-Roman wrestler named Wilfried Dietrich from West Germany. Dietrich was just a little over half the weight of his oversized competitor.

Before the competition, Wilfried walked up to Taylor, the little "David" approaching his "Goliath." But as Taylor reached out to shake his hand, Wilfried brushed it aside and gave the big man a hug. When they wrestled, Wilfried Dietrich hit what was to become the most famous throw in wrestling history. He reached around Chris Taylor, locked his arms and hands around this monster, flipped him onto his head, and pinned him. It turns out that the only reason Dietrich wanted to give Taylor a hug was not because he admired him, but to see if he could get his arms around him. The moral to the story, as Coach Gable told it, was that *winning requires doing all of the right things twenty-four hours a day.*

We have to stay focused. If God has birthed us for a purpose, then we need to live out our purpose 24/7/365. Even if we're just standing around doing nothing, sleeping, just out having fun, at work, vacationing, or shaking someone's hand, our purpose is still focused in our minds. There's something we've been put here to do. People don't lose because the odds are against them. The odds were all against Dietrich when he faced his Goliath. People lose because they lose focus and don't do things right.

We're told that "The steps of a good man are ordered by the Lord, and He delights in his way" (Ps. 37:23). God has marked off a path before you. *Keep your eye on it!* The stone that usually strikes entrepreneurs right in the center of their head and kills dreams and splendid plans is when we take our mind off our money. We do the mission because we want to serve. We keep our mind on our money so we can keep serving.

chapter **8**

LEADERSHIP: BUILDING POWERFUL TEAMS

The secret to successful hiring is this: look for the people who want to change the world.

— *Marc Benioff, CEO of Salesforce*

YOUR MISSION SHOULD BE too big to ignore and too big to do on your own. Your mission-based business requires a mission-based team.

When I first was asked to start consulting, I was perplexed. I did not know precisely why I had seen the success I had and what truly differentiated my business from somebody that wanted my help. I finally reached a point of true sustainability. We were thriving on an unimaginable level day after day, week after week, and were not impacted by any changes in the economy, politics, the seasons, or the weather. But why?

A man that has continued to be a teacher, coach, and mentor in my life, Dr. Mark Chironna, came into my office for help and after he began the program I asked him, "Okay, Dr. Chironna, what worked for you here? What did you experience that caused you to walk in the door and choose us over many other options?" He responded immediately, "Culture vision."

I asked, "What is culture vision?" He explained that everyone he met was "Mini-me." All of the staff in our office embodied my enthusiasm for what we offered, used the same language, and had the same caring tone, he said. There was an overall vision for what was delivered and a commitment to keep delivering it that everyone possessed that permeated the atmosphere.

Candidly, at the time I was not a great leader. On the other hand, I did have an enormous mission and a clear vision for how we could save our community. The mission and the vision were infectious and ubiquitous. As I learned to manage larger and larger teams—which actually took going back to college—employee engagement in the mission became reproducible and predictable. If engagement is there, life is going well. If it is not, there is a different type of infectiousness going about the business and it is not a good one. Mission requires an engaged team to be a success.

THE ONLY REAL PATH TO EMPLOYEE ENGAGEMENT

Becoming one of the top 100 companies to work for is something measured by *Fortune* magazine and other media outlets annually. Today's leading edge companies know that employee satisfaction is the most integral part of their immediate and long-term success. Anyone who has ever run or managed a business knows that the only thing worse than having customer problems is having employee problems. On the other hand, many entrepreneurs, smaller companies, and unfortunately big ones too, only think about the bottom line. Yet, if you're going to really drive mission into your business, it won't just come from the top down, it will come from the bottom up–and out too.

Big companies that are the top 100 best places to work winners, like Apple, Google, or Amazon, obviously have resources we don't, but there is much to learn from their example. These are culture-driven organizations, and cultures change the game.

ORGANIZATIONAL CITIZENSHIP BEHAVIOR (OCB)

OCB is the Heisman of all great leadership rewards. When you create it, your team members are exhibiting an ownership of the mission, promoting excellence in the workplace, going above and beyond the call of duty, taking pride in their work, exhibiting sportsmanship and altruism, and do not need a boss to keep them focused on the task at hand. With OCB, they wear the company T-shirt on the weekends and when they cut themselves, they bleed the corporate colors. This type of employee behavior is so highly valued that there have been numerous studies done to determine the most effective way of creating it. What the examiners tend to find is that nothing matches job satisfaction when it comes to producing OCB.

4 STEPS TO JOB SATISFACTION

For non-billion dollar companies, there are some vital steps to take in order to get your team radically behind your mission and switching their favorite drink to your Kool-Aid.

1. Team first: Put your employees first—ahead of your customers—and your employees will put your customers first. Benefits are important, but great benefits are not always economically viable for start-ups and small companies. Putting your team first is not just a matter of benefits. You can give, but it doesn't mean you give a damn. If team is truly first, you deliver your products or services to them as if they were your most important customer. Rewards, accolades, and recognition are also vital (and covered more in the chapter on Team).

2. Hire culture and skill; not just skill: Different team members in different divisions have different personalities and needs. Hiring the right personality and skill set for the job and making sure that the new hire fits in will make or break the business and the culture. Zappos founder Tony Hsieh says in his book Delivering Happiness that they do not simply hire new employees based on skill, but whether or not a skilled new employee will be a good fit for the culture. Will we get along in the lunch room and at the Christmas party? is an important question.

3. Trust. Great cultures have tackled the enormous monster called healthy communication as a way to create trust. A very common theme among employees that

report they love their work environment is connected to quality, 360-degree communication.

Of the studies on OCB that exist, healthy 360 degrees of communication is at the top of the list. Communication breeds trust and you cannot have commitment without it. 360 degrees is the top-down communication from executives to team members, the bottom-up communication from team members to their managers, and the lateral communication with each other that is well thought out.

Team members need to be part of the planning process for their areas of influence and kept up to speed on the progress, vision, and plans for the future of the organization. Managers with an open-door policy have been shown to build trust far greater than those who sneak into the office and lock the door.

If there is one great rule of lateral communication it is, "No Triangulation"—talking behind someone's back rather than bringing concerns directly to the person. Sportsmanship is another hallmark of OCB, and triangulation is the kind of poor sportsmanship that cannot be tolerated. Similar to a child who throws a tantrum after they lose or mocks others after they win, when it comes to triangulation that dog don't hunt in a winning program.

4. BIG MISSION–OF COURSE! Many if not most of the Top 100 workplaces have a do-good aspect to their game. These mission-based organizations highlight the positive impact their company is making on the planet

and this gets employees out of bed in the morning and excited about coming into the office. You cannot pay enough to replace the enthusiasm that comes with work hard. play hard, do good.

CULTURE IS ATTENTION TO ALL PEOPLE AND PARTS

1 Corinthians 12:24-26 says,

> "God put our bodies together in such a way that even the parts that seem the least important are valuable. He did this to make all parts of the body work together smoothly, with each part caring about the others. If one part of our body hurts, we hurt all over. If one part of our body is honored, the whole body will be happy."

It is easy to see how the people out front contribute to the greater good. But how about the billing and collection team members, data entry, maintenance, and reception? It's like the human body. As Paul is referring to in the passage above, we know you can't live without your heart, but what about one of your fingers? Which one of those are you fine letting go? If you're working at the complaints desk or in accounts payable, you may really struggle to see how what you're doing saves lives. That is not a position issue, that is a leadership issue. Part of the regular training and support process is showing the team members who are not on the front lines how integral their role is to the mission. For example, an employee may be in accounting and never see the client. However, what is the number one reason someone gets upset or never does not commit as a customer? What is the number one reason they will leave you as a customer? It's the money! So who could be more important to the ultimate success of the mission than those in a cubicle paying bills, managing QuickBooks, handling customer account issues, and all of the other unglamorous parts of the company that have everything to do with the mission?

Everyone appreciates the power of the heart to keep their body alive and well. But life also goes bad pretty quickly when the colon or a kidney goes out. All parts are mission-critical and deserving of attention, support, and praise. You do not want any bitter people who quit and stay. You want a growing number of employees whose favorite piece of jewelry is a wristband with your mission statement on it and who don the company logo on Sundays when, no, you're not watching.

THE WALMART MEETING

When Sam's Club/Walmart decided to sell my book in their stores, my publisher flew me out to their famous weekly meeting to speak in front of their executives and managers. While I went there with the expectation of teaching, I learned the administrative lesson of my life. Walmart is the largest and most powerful company in the world due to both its revenues and size with over two million employees. My experience in their weekly meeting helped me understand why and changed my approach to management and team meetings forever. The heads of the departments were assembled in a group next to a PowerPoint projector, in front of the CEO and some other members of his executive team.

One by one the managers stood up and made a presentation to the executives based on the past week's performance of their respective departments and their plans to meet goals the next week. The CEO would comment on the report where necessary and approve or refine their plans. The most impressive parts to me were that the department heads knew their numbers and the level of responsibility they shouldered each week in managing their respective goals.

Here is what each department head report contained:

POINT 1: Celebrate successes and publicly acknowledge and reward key employees that had exhibited remarkable performance or reached a company milestone.

POINT 2: Share what the numbers were for the same week the year before.

POINT 3: Share what the goal was for the week.

POINT 4: Share the actual numbers for the week.

POINT 5: Share the plan.

If on goal: The plan moved forward for continued success.

If off goal: If there was a delta between the actual numbers for the week and the goal, they had to tell the CEO why they believed they fell short and their plan for a solution. After the meeting, I was permitted to ask the CEO one question. I asked, "Why do you have a goal every week?" He responded, "Because by the end of the month we are dead." I was impressed by the responsibility passed on to team members. Most entrepreneurs delegate tasks, but not responsibility. The Walmart managers owned their numbers and were fully responsible for setting the goals, creating the plans to hit them, and for modifications if they were unable to reach the numbers to which they committed. This allowed the leader to lead, rather than be chief cook, and bottle-washer, jack of all trades and master of none.

REQUIREMENTS FOR WALMART-LEVEL DELEGATION

In order to delegate duties in this manner, there are a number of steps. You have to hire quality people that possess the skills and personality to take on the specific job description. There has to be a thorough on-boarding process, training, and on-going support.

AUTHORITARIAN VS. TRANSFORMATIONAL MEETINGS

Like Walmart or any team of any kind, the precision of the meeting is the quintessential practice. Good reporting, a specific set of goals, following and updating the plan, assessing constraints, and clear next steps moving forward are elements of effective weekly meetings. Avoid the type of useless meetings given by authoritarian leaders that consist of long lectures from the man or woman in charge. As I observed at Walmart, the executive team said very little outside of approving or refining the plans moving forward related to managers that needed their support. Helping to refine and support plans of the people given responsibility is part of transformational leadership. People are being transformed into the type of leader they have the potential to become.

A key component of transformational leading is not only allowing errors, but encouraging them. If people are afraid of failure, or working in a punitive culture always looking to place blame, they will not step up as leaders. If you want

Mini-Me's out espousing the virtues of the mission and spreading positive energy throughout the building, they cannot be in fear of a leader's wrath. Failing is good as long as we fail forward.

PERFORMANCE MEASURES

I do not want to sound too touchy-feely or have you miss the point in advocating the benefits of supportive leadership. Going back to the Walmart meeting, managers started their presentation with celebrating successes and employee recognition. But for those that were off-goal for the last several weeks, it was clear that they were in danger of losing their job.

A mean boss that is all authoritarian and transactional and from whom you get a smile only if you hit a home run will create a cold, bitter, anti-mission culture. On the other hand, laissez-faire leadership is lame. A leader can be kind, supportive, and allow for growth and error but teams, individuals, and the company as a whole must make progress and hit goals. If someone has gotten all of the training and support needed to transform and perform and is still unable to hit their numbers, then it should make sense to all that this is not the job for them. In fact, keeping an employee that struggles long-term not only hurts your organization, it hurts their self-esteem, brings others down, and keeps them from finding the mission God created for them.

TEAM MEETING VERSUS TEAM TRAINING

There are two very important parts to team development: weekly team meetings and weekly team trainings.

- Team meetings are a time to discuss concerns, statistics, departments, and what is going on next in the office.

- Team trainings are a time to actually role play scripts and work on office processes and procedures.

Entrepreneurship is neither a science nor an art. It is a practice. —Peter Drucker, management consultant, educator, and author.

A TEAM MEETING MINDSET

- Unify team members by starting out each week on the same page.

- Enable team members to establish and sustain accountability by reporting on their departments.

- Empower team members to be solutions-driven for self, team, and mission growth.

STEPS TO HIRING (BUS LOADING)

In his book *Good to Great*, Jim Collins coined the now well-known concept, "Get the right people on the bus." At the time I read that, it certainly seemed simple enough. The reality of it was that I had to actually go back to college to learn the complexities of bus loading. It had become fairly clear that there was something wrong with the bus driver–me.

Collins also says in *Good to Great* that you must not only get the right people on the bus, but that you also need to have the right people in the right seats, and the wrong people off the bus. This is a very intentional process and not done by feeling or desperation, as is so often the case. Most businesses do not take this process seriously until having and keeping good people has become a crisis. Here are the basic steps, and you may never need to know much more.

1. THE INTERVIEW.

There are unstructured and structured interviews.

Unstructured interview:

- When you hire someone because they seem to be the right fit for the job, you like them, and they were the most qualified of those that answered your ad.

Structured interview:

- You determine KSOAs (Knowledge, Skills, Abilities, and Other competencies) necessary to do the work based on a specific job description.

- You establish a way to measure their personality and aptitude for the job by using one of the personality instruments described below.

- Set up an activity center for the applicants to participate in that mirrors required job skills.

- They are only considered a candidate if they meet these specifications.

- You call their list of references.

BOX: Personality profiling is the godfather of all valid predictors of performance

There is high validity related to the use of personality profiles in determining future job performance. The most generally accepted personality model is the Five-Factor Model. For this model, it has been extremely well established that there is a relationship between success and personality performance across all occupations.

The Five-Factor model

The Five-Factor model has five main dimensions and sub-groups or sub-dimensions that accompany each that more deeply describe the trait. The five main dimensions are Neuroticism, Extroversion, Openness to Experience, Agreeableness, and Conscientiousness.

While personality traits are very connected to job performance and are able to consistently performance. An area, for example, that relates particularly well to personality is in evaluating sales personnel. Therefore, as in any job role, knowing the best traits to choose from when hiring someone for sales can be highly advantageous for sales-dependent organizations.

Using the Five-Factor model to predict and hire for sales success

The **Conscientiousness** trait indicates people that are disciplined, self-controlled, strategic planners, and work to carry out goals. Conscientiousness is the dimension that ties the heaviest of all dimensions with job performance and is the gold standard across all roles and occupations. For sales, workers who are rated in this dimension are also the most likely to perform and get high marks from management.

Neuroticism refers to individuals who tend to be shy, angry, insecure, depressed, vulnerable, introverted, and anxious. Thus, this trait pairs terribly in a sales job. On the other hand, **extroversion** is a personality trait connected to being sociable, talkative, and people-oriented. As a result it makes sense that extroverted sales personnel will outperform their neurotic, introverted counterparts.

Openness to Experience refers to individuals who tend to be creative, imaginative, and curious to experience new things. Even though Conscientiousness is considered to be the top Big Five predictor of job performance, Openness is important and is measurably favored for sales, as they tend to put more compassion and emotion into what can become monotone, scripted work.

The sum of the above in creating a structured interview process for a sales-oriented position equates to looking for results in a personality profile of Conscientiousness, Extroversion, and Openness to Experience. If someone does not rank strongly in all or most of these areas on their personality test, then they are not right for the job.

The instruments of personality, behavior, strength, and style. It's important to know what individual tests are actually measuring and what good they've been proven to offer. Common tests that measure different components of a person's makeup and predict performance are the Myers-Briggs Type Indicator (MBTI), DISC, and the Clifton StrengthsFinder. MBTI focuses on personality type, the

DISC looks at behavior, and StrengthsFinder focuses on talents and style.

Example: The D.I.S.C. Profile

Different positions in the office require different skills, strengths, and personality profiles. Generally, if you are high in one you are low in others. They key is a balanced organization possessing individuals strong in personality traits specific to their area of work.

DISC Personality Profile

D: Dominance
I: Influence
S: Steadiness
C: Compliance

Hiring and Positioning Using the D.I.S.C.

High D's are driven and possess strong leadership skills

High I's are personality and relationship focused

High S's are loyal and supportive

High C's are your detail, number oriented programmers, data entry people, and bookkeepers.

Utilizing personality profiles is a skill. There are many organizations that provide these materials for you at a modest cost. That small investment will pay dividends in performing employees down the road.

2. EATING THE ONBOARDING, TRAINING, AND SUPPORT ELEPHANT

When a new team member begins, I want them to feel that the job will be fun, inspiring, and that they can fairly easily and successfully master the work. I want them going home excited and encouraged, not overwhelmed and saying, "I'll never learn it!" This is the "What is the best way to eat an elephant?" method: one bite at a time. Give them small bits and bites that they can easily digest so that every training day is a win.

Onboarding refers to the process of integrating new employees into the organization, of preparing them to succeed at their job, and to become fully engaged, productive members of the health care organization. Studies have shown that a well-designed onboarding program can turn a new hire into a dedicated employee, reducing the costs of turnover.

The onboarding orientation is a time when new employees are told the organization's history and traditions, and where they become familiar with the foundation behind the movement, the values, philosophy, culture, language, and vision of the company.

Training: It is not "train yourself" or just "shadow another employee" only. A playbook with all scripts and processes they will be accountable for should be handed to them along with the bite-sized chunks and order they are expected to learn.

Support: Employees and managers should be assigned to them to make sure they are moving through training at a healthy pace and get them plugged into weekly meetings and trainings.

CAUTION

Every employer comes to despise the work and cost that goes into a new employee. But the only thing harder and more expensive is skipping steps in the process and not doing it well. There is little worse in business then losing employees and starting over and over again because the bus driver keeps doing a poor job putting the right people on the bus! In health care, the annual turnover rate according to the Human Resource Management Association is 20.4 percent. That means one in five quit their jobs each year. A new nurse, for example, costs over $50,000 to recruit and train. To replace an experienced critical care nurse can cost as much $120,000. Your costs may be much lower or higher. On top of the costs, there may be no worse life-ruining, business-related stress than a team that is unhappy, non-performing, and falling apart. The time and energy invested into good hiring and support processes is all ROI.

BONUSES

You cannot have a performance-based environment without people experiencing some type of meritocracy. The vast majority of my working adult life has been only miles from the Walt Disney World companies in Orlando, Florida. As a result, I have always had to figure out why you should come and stay working for me rather than going to work for the Mouse: it is not easy to compete with free park passes, discounted stays at hotels, and 15 percent off all Disney gear, mouse-ears and all!

My greater focus has been on a mission to save lives, but people want to be fairly compensated for their efforts too and know they have the potential to thrive financially. My position has been that if, as a result of our collective efforts or your individual work, the mission makes more money, then you should make more money too. That is different than Disney, the law firm paying an extra dollar an hour around the corner, or another big company with a better lunch room. If you want people to really take ownership, then they should be able to see the numbers as well as see additional pay for their growth.

All businesses, large and small, have departments. Even if there's only two of you working at a Sun Glass Hut, there is a new customer department, customer service, accounts payables, and accounts receivables. Each department, like at Walmart, has a leader with a goal and a plan. If those goals are reached, there should be additional compensation, particularly if you want to incentivize someone to keep reaching, keep planning, and to continue to hit goals.

SIMPLE BONUS METHODS

In the case of the Sun Glass Hut, the employee in charge of total glasses sold could get $100 if the goal was achieved. For the employee in charge of reaching a total collections of $50,000 for the month, they may get $500 for hitting a large money-based goal such as that one.

The key to healthy bonusing is just making sure that you set goals that work within the confines of your particular economic model. You want to be jumping for joy, hugging, and high-fiving your team as you pass out bonus checks because you all just won the World Series. You don't want to be frowning because you had to take money out of operating capital or your personal dividends to cover the loss.

I personally like the ownership-thinking model of bonusing best. You create a profit baseline, then take 5-10 percent of profits above that and divide it out among the staff in order of job significance, position, and level in the company. This gets them thinking like an owner and you're protected because they only get it based on profit.

FOR THE OWNERSHIP-THINKING BONUS SYSTEM

In our Sun Glass Hut, if the minimum profit you want to take home is $10,000, then the employee(s) only get paid on profits over and above. Thus, if you collected $50,000 and your overhead is $25,000 you are left with a profit of $25,000. This is $15,000 over your $10,000 baseline. This results in employees sharing a percentage of $15,000. If the number was 10 percent they share $1,500 and you make an additional $13,500 ($15,000 less $1,500). You are up $13,500 and they are up their share of $1,500 and everyone parties like they just won the World Series!

chapter 8

PLANNING AND GOAL SETTING

Give me a stock clerk with a goal and I'll give you a man who will make history. Give me a man with no goals and I'll give you a stock clerk.

—*James Cash, (JC) Penney.*

GOING FROM WHERE YOU ARE TO WHERE YOU WANT TO BE

REVISIT YOUR DREAM. What have you changed or abandoned? What songs, books, paintings, businesses, purposes, inventions, and intentions have you left behind so long ago that you almost don't dare to think about them again? You need to begin believing once again that:

1. Your dreams are authentic and important. They are put in your heart by God.

2. You're not powerless, worthless, or hopeless. You have great value and significance.

3. What's inside of you is more powerful than any circumstance.

4. More importantly, Who's inside you is more powerful than any problem in front of you.

5. Turbulence, chaos, ambiguity, and change are not there to stop you. They are there to strengthen, shape, mold, and ultimately help you.

TELEOLOGICAL GOAL SETTING

In John 19:28 just before dying on the cross, Jesus said, "tetelestai" which means, "It is finished." Jesus was and still is a finisher.

Finishing or teleological acts are those that lock on their target like the heat-seeking sensors on a missile: they don't stop no matter what resistance comes to deceive them or knock them off course. They hit their target anyway. If you aim a gun at a target and pull the trigger, once the bullet leaves the gun you have no control as to where it will land. With a heat-seeking missile, once you've locked on the target, no matter how much turbulence occurs or how evasive the target gets, it will course correct as often as is necessary to reach its goal.

Absent a destination, any road will take you there. Goals give you a destination, and whether you think you have them or not, you do. If in your mind you consider yourself to be a C student, a lower-level employee, a nonathlete, a fat and depressed old person, and so on, then believe it or not, because you're teleological, you'll achieve those very goals. You're aimed at failure, and what's worse, you're hitting the target right on the bull's-eye! On the other hand, if you have rich and powerful goals, you're teleologically aimed at winning. You're a guided missile! What's great is that you're locked on to hit those targets now or later. If the goals are clear, tangible, visible, vivid, and well-planned, you are literally spiritually designed to hit them.

STEPS TO GOAL SETTING

Goals are for the purpose of something. Purposes define who we are as individuals.

Determine your priorities, which are the spokes on your "wheelof life":

- Spiritual

- Family

- Fitness

- Physical health

- Personal development

- Financial

- Your purpose

- Fun/trips/possessions

Create a one-year, five-year, and ten-year vision for each of these priorities.

A VISION WITH A DEADLINE IS A GOAL

Develop *big, audacious visions* with near-term, attainable, deadline-driven goals. A vision with a deadline is a goal.

Each goal you achieve should move you closer and *closer* to the vision.

List what you'll create goals for. You must be specific with each of the spokes on your wheel of life or you'll have a lop-sided wheel. You can't just have a family goal. There has to be a goal for you and your spouse, you and individual children, and you and individual extended family members. Create a vivid, clear picture. Were the details specific enough?

For example, if you want a house, do you have the details down that explain the landscaping, the bricks paving the driveway, the flooring, the window coverings, the furniture, the colors, where the kids will play, and where you'll make memories?

Develop a plan. It's not "think it and ink it." Faith is a fact, and faith is an act. What prayerfully prepared plan do you have to reach the goals in the timeframe you've set? This includes:

- Who will help you?

- Where/how will you get the resources?

- What type and order of steps need to be taken?

The plan is then brought down to ground level by going into your to-do lists and ending up in your war plan.

GOAL SETTING

S.M.A.R.T. GOALS. Goals should be:

S - Specific

M - Measurable

A - Achievable

R - Relevant

T - Time Phased

As you'll see next, these are scheduled out monthly, quarterly, and annually. It should always be crystal clear where you want to be in a month, a quarter, and a year. Ultimately, you also want to be clear on where you will be in 3-5 years. Managing your company through SMART goals takes your vision and give you all direction. When the Bible says, "Without vision the people perish" (Prov 29:18). The word perish means to "cast off restraint." They lose focus or run around like chickens with their heads cut off. A vision built on SMART goals give focus, restraint, the direction needed not only have a vision but achieve a vision.

CORPORATE: THE ONE-YEAR STRATEGIC PLAN

THE ONE-YEAR STRATEGIC PLAN

Trite, but true—fail to plan and you plan to fail. The best industry leaders can tell you where their company is headed in three to five years. Then, everything happening this quarter is based on landing at that space in three to five years. If you haven't locked in on the future, then there may not be much sense as to what is happening today.

To be great and sane, you need a one-year strategic plan at a minimum. By fixing points at the end of the year, you can break it down into what has to happen each quarter. By knowing your quarters, you create a plan for each month–which directs the weeks and days as well.

THE GAP ANALYSIS

If the goal is to be collecting $100,000 a month in a year and you are at $20,000 right now, then the gap is $80,000. This gap is represented by certain gaps in marketing, sales, technology, points of execution, and others. Once you have set your two points:

Where we are now ---------------------**Where we want to be**

(GAP)

Marketing	Marketing
Sales	Sales
Technology	Technology
Current team members	Skilled technicians

In a year, we want to have closed that gap if we plan to be at the $100,000 a month point. But, you cannot do it all over night. The process is deciding the foundational baseline to start for the first quarter and determining what benchmarks need to be hit and how you will advance quarter by quarter.

Here is an oversimplified way of laying this out. You can go to gazelles.com or read Verne Harnish's book, *Mastering the Rockefeller Habits*, to learn more about one-year strategic plans and gain more resources.

(GAP = TENSION)

WHERE YOU ARE ---------- WHERE YOU WANT TO BE

MIT's Peter Senge, author of *The Fifth Discipline*, states, "The gap causes creative tension. If you push through the resistance related to the learning curve of growth, you are pushed to learn, develop, invent, and innovate."

ANNUAL GOAL: $100,000 a month in collections (along with other business and financial goals)

Quarter 1 (Q1) goals: Choose no more than two or three arenas to conquer per quarter

1.

2.

3.

Tactics necessary for each month to land at Q1 goals:

-

-

-

Q2

1.

2.

3.

Tactics necessary for each month to land at Q 2 goals:

-

-

-

Q3

1.

2.

3.

Tactics necessary for each month to land at Q3 goals:

-

-

-

Q4

1.

2.

3.

Tactics necessary for each month to land at Q4 goals:

-

-

-

chapter 9

WAR PLANNING

"It's not the will to win that matters—everyone has that. It's the will to prepare to win that matters."

—*Paul "Bear" Bryant*

TIME MANAGEMENT

YOU CAN'T WIN WITHOUT a strategy or plan. Great coaches have great playbooks and great game plans. A successful pilot has a flight plan or he won't reach his destination. A great general must have a war plan or he'll never win the war. I'm going to give you a winning war plan.

As busy as people are, mostly they're not busy fulfilling their purposes—they're just busy. The apostle Paul warns us, "Be very careful, then, how you live—not as unwise but as wise, making the most of every opportunity, because the days are evil" (Eph. 5:15-16). I like how some translations of Ephesians 5:16 say, "Redeem the time."

You need to realize that time is either working for you or against you. Perhaps this is clearest when it comes to health. When an unhealthy, unhappy person walks into one of our offices, they've built up some level of "Medical Sick Debt." Medications, sugars, a lack of fitness, and an abused, degenerating spine make every day evil in that they are another day closer to disease and early death. On the other hand, once they decide to really value their body and invest the time, energy, and money into their good health, they've now gone from living unwise to living wise. They begin paying off their health debt, investing in their health, and now every day they're getting wellness dividends in return. They've redeemed evil days for good ones.

If you live long enough, eventually you're going to die. But, you may be surprised at how well you can do from fifty to over one hundred. I've seen people who had heart disease or cancer in their fifties decide to start living wise and making time work for them rather than against them. As a result, they find themselves healthier than they've ever been. You can get older and *healthier* instead of just older. It is the same with money: When you have debt, time is working against you. When you have investments, time is working for you.

Everyone's busy. People are speeding through life, going from birth to death as fast as they can. They're not walking through the valley of the shadow of death; they're galloping through it! Even our retirees at our businesses tell us that the reason they miss or come late to appointments at our offices is because they're so busy. You want to ask them, "Busy? You're retired. What did you have—a board meeting or something?"

With society experiencing more sickness, obesity, depression, family dysfunction, war, and financial problems than ever, the big thing you have to wonder is, "What is everyone so busy doing?" *We are busier than we are successful!* You see it all of the time: a person who is unhealthy, unfit, unhappy, and broke constantly on their cell phone. The next time you see someone like this, ask them, "Who is that you're talking to (or texting)?" Then say, "If that's not the president, your pastor, your personal trainer, or your financial planner, then hang up (or stop typing). In fact, drop and give me twenty!"

LIFE-TIME MANAGEMENT

It is incredibly common to build a business and lose your life. I have had to remind clients hundreds of times over that their family is the mission. Managing your minutes and your moments allows you to have your cake and eat it too.

MANAGING YOUR TIME

Managing your time is perhaps the most significant aspect of managing your life. If you had forty-eight hours a day to get things done instead of twenty-four, your stress would already be reduced, you'd double your customer base, you'd eat less fast food, and you'd probably even exercise more. Although it may not appear that way right now, this is possible. The time is there, all you have to do is get twice as much use out of it.

Much of your time is centered around handling all the issues and "emergencies" you face with your relationships, your health, your work, and your stressful outlook on life. In a life like that, you end up so focused on just getting *through your day* that you forget about getting *from your day.* The result of that kind of focus is more issues and "emergencies" that use up even more time.

The following time management section will show you how to organize and strategize your time so it is focused on activities that build a healthy, happy, peaceful, and successful life. This is the key to stress management, relationship building, financial increase, appearance enhancement, and health control.

Time management "over time" will create less and smaller issues and emergencies, allowing you to continue focusing more of your time on what you are passionate about and what and who is important.

IS TIME OWNING YOU OR ARE YOU OWNING YOUR TIME?

Typically, *you are not managing your time; it is managing you.* In fact, the constant crises and deadlines of your thoroughly modern day are most likely determining your each and every move—and managing your time, your body, and your emotions.

When you woke up this morning, it is likely that the very first things you thought of were not those things necessary to create time for exercise, better nutrition, and peace from God. Instead, from the moment you opened your eyes, you were probably thinking of those things that were so vital they had to be handled *immediately.* As time went on, you most likely spent the rest of your day handling urgent issues, meeting deadlines, managing relationship breakdowns, and attempting to get to places *on time.*

Most people would consider this "effective" time management. They have organized their day so the most important and pressing issues are being handled first, and so they are not late to anything.

However, this is not really "time management," it is "emergency management." In emergency management, your *time* manages *you*. Rather than getting from the day, you are getting through the day. Most people have four activities that could be full-time jobs. To do all the things you do *full-time*, you really need to get 160 hours out of a 40-hour work week. Work mission, ministry, family fitness, hobbies, and plans for the future all deserve quality, focused time. The truth is that all people *have* the time, they just don't know how to *manage* the time effectively. "With the Lord a day is like a thousand years, and a thousand years are like a day" (2 Pet. 3:8). You may not be able to get up to a thousand hours out of a day, but with the right strategy you can get more done in a week, with more peace than you ever thought possible.

DISCIPLINE IS FREEDOM?

Discipline sounds like confinement, but it is the opposite. As they say, "Only those with the discipline to practice the violin are FREE to play beautiful music." That metaphor goes for any discipline in life–with it comes freedom to express your gifts and talents.

Mission is not like playing a video game, smoking pot, drinking beer, eating fast food, and hanging out at the mall. These things may give some temporary pleasure, but never provide satisfaction. The only true, permanent joy and absolute, total freedom is found in Mission Work. The life that is inspired and obedient to God is the blessed life. It is a life that goes beyond simple happiness into an inner sense of peace and fulfillment. Schedule your time—and become free!

THE ART OF WAR PLANNING

War planning is the tool in the toolbox necessary to pull your whole life together. While never the sexiest part of my books, lectures, or consulting, it is easily the most important. Master this section and you can master anything.

ARE YOU BUSIER THAN YOU ARE SUCCESSFUL?

If you're busy but your relationships, fitness levels, and bank accounts aren't growing, then you are busier than you are successful. Wouldn't it be great to be more successful than you are busy? To rush and stress less, yet have more? Well, it's completely possible if you'll be wise and exchange bad "man time" for good "God time." The days are evil. It's truly an upside-down world. Priorities that should be at the top are at the bottom, and the ones that should be at the bottom are at the top. Changing this won't happen by accident. It's going to take a war to redeem what you're busy doing for what you should be doing, and because of that you need a winning war plan.

PLANNING 101: WRITE IT DOWN!

Perhaps the most painful, serotonin-depleting (depression-causing) life management mistake you can make is what we call "memory management." Memory management is simply trying to remember everything you have to do. It's the most literal interpretation there is of making mountains out of molehills. Memory management will turn a week of errands into climbing Mt. Everest—*in a blizzard.* It's a losing strategy! There are two necessary terms I use to show you how to best lay out your path in order to climb it more easily and successfully. *The written to-do list:* This is a written list that lets you see exactly what to do and eliminates memory management. All the action steps required to meet your goals are written down here.

The war plan: The war plan is when you convert the to-do list, the Battle Strategies" we will cover, and your fixed schedule into a weekly action plan. You take what has to be done and give it a specific day, time, and duration in order to accomplish it without worry.

THE WRITTEN TO-DO LIST

The written to-do list is simple and self-explanatory. It's planning 101, really: write it down. Nothing should be stored only in a mental file. Make out a list at the beginning of each week either in a planner, an electronic planner, a computer file marked "To-do for the week of_____," or a calendar, or do it old school in a notebook. This is an absolute minimum for living with any degree of success or sanity.

AVOID "LOOSE PAPER SYNDROME!" Loose paper syndrome is an actual term in psychology for the stress, anxiety, and sleeplessness caused by writing to-do notes all over the place on stickies, napkins, backs of folders, yellow legal pads, and all of the other remote places that are tough to find later. Whether it is an old school note pad or a new school digital device, write it down in one reliable, findable place.

THE WINNING WAR PLAN

Win the battles and the war.

You're in a daily war, fighting against the manifestations of a world system that is opposed to God—things like disease, debt, emotional turmoil, weight gain, shrinking muscles, divorce, and failed relationships. If you're a parent, you're also fighting against all of the enemies your children have to face that would block their health and future.

No matter how badly you want to win, you can't win a game, much less a war, without a strategic plan of attack. Without a winning war plan, you will lose the battles and, in the end, the whole war. The will to win is not nearly as important as the will to prepare to win. In fact, if you have a big desire or will to win but have not acquired the skill to win, you'll just have big frustration.

How many people, despite so much on the line, go into a day or week with a strategic plan? Maybe one or two percent of the population? Make sure you're in that one or two percent—have a plan. The Winning War Plan is your to-do list along with your fixed schedule, like school or work, along with Battle Strategies needed to go from $0 - $1,000,000. broken up into what days and times each task is going to happen, as well as how much time to *just do it.*

THE BATTLE STRATEGIES

The more you sweat in training, the less you bleed in battle.
—Navy SEAL motto.

There is the war and then there are the battles you have to win to win the war. When we are war planning, we maximize the amount of time focused on these strategies so that time spent is mission advancing. Many of these strategies are YOU – based as your performance, energy, and social well-being weighs heavily on the ability to grow many types of companies.

Battle Strategies include: Healthy Lifestyle, Relationship Building, Spiritual Growth, Social and Community Development, Skill Sharpening and New Skill Development, Opportunities, Planning and Organization, Goal Setting, Launching, Getting Coaching, Masterminding, Sharpening the Axe, and Maintenance.

Mission Work is working *on* your life rather than just reacting to the stress trouble, and emergencies that are in your life.

HEALTHY LIFESTYLE

You're no good to God, your family, or your mission if you're sick or dead. Any information or activity designed to move you toward your ultimate health potential by maximizing the natural strengths, fitness level, and appearance of your body and its God-given ability to heal.

RELATIONSHIP BUILDING

Prioritizing time for family, friends, business associates, and cultural groups on a regular basis in order to create communication, trust, better ideas, teamwork, unity, conflict resolution, and lasting relationships.

This includes Date Time. To avoid the stress of relationship emergencies, time in the principal's office, and the pain and expense of corporate and divorce attorneys, it is critical to work on building your relationships frequently with your spouse, children, girl-/boyfriend, relatives, close friends, and important business associates.

Pick a morning, afternoon, or evening and schedule a special time with the people who are important to you. Each person gets their own date and their own time. People like your spouse and children get a date time at the same or similar time every week with a solid yellow line surrounding—and protecting—it. For a fire to survive, the logs cannot stand alone. Logs burn longer, brighter, and hotter when they are surrounded by other logs. An incredibly important part of your week in which to spend committed, compartmentalized energy is in the building of your relationships. All health and peace will fail if your relationships are falling apart, and no money or success is as important as the people in your world.

Few of us spend near as much time building our basic human relationships as we should. As a result, we lose a lot of time and sleep dealing with relationship emergencies. Relationship emergencies can become the most stressful part of our existence and will completely debilitate any chance at having a Life by God.

Relationship emergencies usually come from a lack of communication. For instance, there is a young married couple who have not communicated enough due to the brevity of their relationship and the fact that they are both very busy with work. One night, the young man comes home late, goes to get a drink of water and sees that there is a glass in the sink that his wife left there three days ago. He then thinks to himself that she does that all the time and he really hates that. Tired and in a bad mood, he chooses right then to ask his wife why she does not put glasses in the dishwasher after she uses them.

Realizing she always does that and he must have been unhappy with this for months, she gets very upset and decides to tell him about a thing or two she hates. The end result is a massive relationship emergency due to lack of communication.

Relationship building/communication times with business partners, employees, relatives, friends, spouses, and children are vital parts in your week to paint solid yellow lines around. This will stop marriages and business relationships from going from the honeymoon to the courtroom, keep your kids out of counseling and principals' offices, and help you continue to get invited to your aunt's house for Thanksgiving.

The best way to assure regular interaction with the people in your life who are important to you is to schedule date times. Date times are time slots you etch in stone at some point each week—morning, afternoon, or night—when you and someone you wish to build and maintain a solid, committed relationship with can enjoy some time together.

Your spouse and individual children get time each week, and your close friends, relatives, and important business associates get time at least monthly. Each child and adult should get their own date time. Do not put them all in a room one day a week and call it "mission accomplished."

Date times are things like breakfast out with your spouse right after the kids are dropped off at school every Tuesday morning, your child's favorite movie or video every Thursday night, dinner with your best friend or important business associate every third Monday at 7:00 p.m. , or a call to your aunt in Alaska every Friday at noon!

Though one may be overpowered, two can defend themselves. —Ecclesiastes 4:11

A LESSON FROM DAD: MOMENT MANAGEMENT

At the age of fifty-two, my father died suddenly and without warning. The unexpected shock of his death and his early departure from the planet left me feeling bitter for a couple of years. What finally got me past the feeling that I had been shortchanged or somehow ripped off was looking back on my life and realizing that I'd had a lot of good "moments" with my dad over the time of his short life.

My father was your classic late-twentieth-century working dad. Even though he was gone before I got up for school and came home late for dinner every night, I always had tremendous respect and appreciation for him.

I respected how hard he worked, that he was great at his job, and that he had reached several positions of authority. I appreciated the fact that, although we were not rich, we never wanted for anything. When he walked in the door at the end of the day, my little brothers and I were not just happy to see him, we were jumping out of our skin, bouncing off of the walls.

As hard as my father worked, and as focused as he was, never for a second did I feel neglected. The reason I always felt loved and appreciated was that while most of his week was consumed by work, when we were together we had endless good "moments."

I truly do not remember being without my dad, but I totally remember everything about being with my dad. The games, the catches, the wrestling matches, the car rides, vacations, movies, meals, lectures about life, and the time when I was in college and he drove four hours to surprise me at a bus station so I wouldn't have to take the bus home, are all "moments" that are indelibly carved into my brain and my spirit forever.

The quality of your life is not measured by the amount of time you spend, it is measured by the amount of "moments" you have in it. You should have many "lives"—Business Life, Purpose Life, Spiritual Life, Student Life, Husband/Wife or Boy/Girlfriend Life, and Dad or Mom Life. The quality and effectiveness of these "lives" will be determined by the focus and energy you put into the "moments" within these "lives" rather than just the time you spend on them.

I wish I had my dad another 30 years. Yet, when I reflect back on my childhood and early adulthood, I thank God for the many incredible "moments" He allowed my dad and I to share before He took my dad home.

SPIRITUAL GROWTH

Inspirational Time. Along with being educational, certain books, audios, videos, and speakers can be inspirational.

Exposing yourself and your family to inspirational multi-media as opposed to the many other types of negative materials that are available keeps you and those around you positive and inspired.

This involves time with God. This is time spent praying, listening, and reading in order to move closer to God and cause greater spiritual understanding and growth.

SPIRITUAL TRIATHLON: TRAIN LIKE A CHAMPION

A typical triathlon in sports is a race where you swim, bike, and run. Winning a triathlon takes elite physical conditioning only found through consistent training focused on the three disciplines of the sport. In life and for eternity, the most important win is to win in your relationship with God. It's a race you just can't allow yourself to lose. Like any relationship, it takes focused effort. That's why Paul tells a young Timothy, "Train yourself to be godly" (1 Tim. 4:7).

When it comes to knowing God, you want to train like a champion. To do so requires a daily "spiritual triathlon."

This triathlon consists of three disciplines:

• Bible time (reading *about* God and words *from* God)

• Prayer time (speaking to God)

• Quiet time (listening to God)

BIBLE—READING TIME

Read your Bible or a devotional reading. Volume is great, but often quality reading, where you really read for comprehension and memory, works as well or better.

PRAYER—TALK TO GOD TIME

Pray, but don't talk in old-style English with Him. He's a good Father, and He's your Father. Talk to Him like someone you know and love. He loves to hear from you.

QUIET—LISTENING TIME

After speaking with Him and gaining insight through His word, listen for His quiet voice. Modern society is a loud, concrete jungle. Whether you're in the developed world or the two-thirds world, chances are your world is filled with television, cell phones, and throngs of people driving and walking down paved roads and sidewalks in commercial and housing developments that used to be fields and forests. This "modern" and "advanced" living allows for no quiet, peaceful time in nature. This makes it very difficult to really hear, see, and, especially, feel the presence of God. That's why it's so important to make the time to "be still and know that I am God" (Ps. 46:10, emphasis added). I have found the only way to get consistent, good quality time with God and truly give Him your best is if you do it first thing in the morning—before your day and everyone else's day starts racing on.

I know the excuse already, "I'm not a morning person."

The truth is, however, if you're a "go-to-bed-on-time person," 5:00–6:00 a.m. doesn't come so early, especially if you go to bed at or before 10:00 p.m. I know you're doing really important things at 10:00 p.m.—like watching American Idol (aka "American Idle") or Facebooking, but I believe you'll find that the time with God is far more transforming than the time with Ryan Seacrest or looking at someone else's vacation photos.

I know the other excuse already, too: "I don't have time for anything more." One thing you'll never hear anyone say is, "Boy, I wish I hadn't spent all of that time with God this morning. It really messed up my day." Time with God allows you to nurture the most important relationship in your life. I guarantee that whatever time you take with Him will be given back to you many times over! You can do your spiritual triathlon in as little as fifteen minutes—that's just five minutes for each discipline. Would more time be better? Possibly. Yet, if you did your spiritual triathlon every day because you had time versus hardly ever doing it because you believe you don't have the time, you're obviously far better off doing it fifteen minutes every day.

SOCIAL AND COMMUNITY INVOLVEMENT

Remember, the success of any organization is dependent on the success its leader has with the leaders of other organizations. In addition to be an accelerant to building your business, getting out to co-mission is also part of time employed meeting your moral obligations to enhance the community and lighten the burden of others. This is accomplished by working with corporate, educational, religious, charitable, fraternal, and other community organizations.

SKILL SHARPENING AND NEW SKILL DEVELOPMENT

Spending time learning and developing new skills to enhance your value in the areas you are already involved in or becoming effective in new areas. In this type of work, you are enhancing and mastering your skills and abilities so you are always moving toward your God-given potential in all areas of your life.

This includes big time educational time. Time spent learning the latest technology in your area of expertise, expanding your knowledge base to new areas of proficiency, and exposing yourself to information on how to live a peaceful, successful, and purposeful life make up Educational Time.

This time of personal growth and self-empowerment is critical to your continued spiritual growth and maturity. Time alone does not create growth, Educational Time does. Otherwise, the older people got the happier they would be, and this is usually not the case.

Committing to finish books, audios, and videos, signing up for classes and seminars, and scheduling coaching and masterminding time should be a consistent part of your schedule.

Continue to get better at what you do, and learn to do new things. The world is ever advancing. The number one reason for failure in business, health, and relationships is simply "staying the same."

Only the mediocre think they are always at their best. You are either growing or dying. Putting time into sharpening your skills and developing new proficiencies will keep you on top of things and better able to adapt to a constantly developing world.

OPPORTUNITIES

Seeking out and/or *creating* personal and business opportunities. Looking at new possibilities and making them a focused part of the plan makes sure you go through the doors God opens before they close. As the saying goes, "*He who deliberates too long before taking a step spends his life on one foot.*" When it is *time* to move, you need to be prepared to move.

PLANNING AND ORGANIZATION

The Battle Strategy in the war plan that is about the war plan. Planning your day, week, month, year, or years has to be in the time management plan. Plus, putting time into your employee meetings by revising the playbook, preparing for training, and looking at the stats will mean just about everything to your future.

Goal-Setting

Without goals, you are traveling without a compass *or* a destination. You have to be consciously focused on a bull's-eye in order to achieve your desired results. Set apart time every week, month, and year for organizing your goals.

Setting and resetting goals is as important to your survival and success as it is to breathing in and out. Writing down goals is also a tremendous act of faith. It shows that you are believing in God to bring the very things He has placed in your heart to write down. Remember, faith is the substance of things hoped for, so write down your SMART goals and have faith that they are as real as the pen you are writing with or the seat you are sitting in.

Launching

Going forth into personal and business communities and exposing yourself to more of what is out there will give you the potential to find new opportunities and be upwardly mobile in *all* areas of your life.

After all, if you don't get the bat off your shoulder, how will you ever be a hit? Opportunity Time is not waiting for your ship to come in, it is launching your own ship.

GETTING COACHING

There is no great athlete, composer, business leader, or religious leader who did not have a great teacher. The fastest, least painful way to the top is to have someone show you the quickest, easiest way.

I have coaches for everything. I have spiritual coaches, marriage coaches, health coaches, parenting coaches, financial coaches, sports coaches, and business coaches. Rarely do I make important decisions in my life without consulting some of these people.

My coaches are also the people I spend my time with. These are the people with whom I choose to eat dinner and go on vacation. I do this because when I am with them I am made a better person. These people sharpen my ax. They make me more capable of moving through life as a sharpened ax is able to move through wood—cleaner, easier, and more effectively.

I don't even personally know some of my coaches. They are authors, lecturers, and business leaders. I go to their seminars, listen to their tapes, and study their organizations as a way of continuing to motivate myself and get even sharper.

Learning and being coached by others who have achieved a higher level of success than you have achieved, particularly in areas you participate in or would like to participate in. You can be coached in sports, business, and relationships with your spouse, with your children, and with God.

1. Coaching Focus: Many things of which a wise man might choose to be ignorant.

Masterminding

Masterminding means meeting with people who **have** goals and beliefs similar to yours so you may reap the benefits of the wisdom of others as well as the benefits of a team effort toward meeting those goals.

Sharpen the Ax

Webinars, teleseminars, brick and mortar seminars, podcasts, videos, and any other way you can consume content that allows you to get sharper. If you are too busy for any of this, then you are too busy. Re-focusing, training, or sharpening the axe is critical on some kind of weekly, bi-weekly, monthly, or quarterly basis. It's pretty clear; "If the ax is dull and its edge unsharpened, more strength is needed but skill will bring success" (Eccl. 10:10).

2. Maintenance

Regularly caring for your body, your possessions, and your relationships so they continue to function at their optimum level and do not break down or need replacing.

Prevention Time

Maintaining mechanical and technical equipment is crucial to avoiding many emergencies. Spending time without transportation due to a broken-down car, waiting in repair shops, or going to the store to replace equipment is incredibly stressful and can be entirely avoided with proper maintenance of your possessions. While taking care of your things may seem hard or time-consuming while you are doing it, it will be easier, less stressful, and time-saving in the long run. True freedom and prosperity can only come when your life's work is your mission. Then you never work another day in your life.

The Elements of the Winning War Plan

The basic structure of the Winning War Plan is generally the fixed part: church, school, work hours, and lunch usually are the same every week. Ultimately, you need to redeem some of what you normally do by eliminating it in exchange for the Battle Strategies.

Every week, at the same time, have specific time set aside for faith, family, fitness, and some of the Battle Strategies for personal and business development. If you're busy then your employees, business, relationships, body, and finances should all be getting better and your mission should be advancing. Do this right, and you'll be more successful than you are busy.

PUTTING THE WINNING WAR PLAN-TOGETHER: CREATING SOLID YELLOW BOXES

What does it take to be a successful entrepreneur? It takes willingness to learn, to be able to focus, to absorb information, and to always realize that business is a 24/7 job where someone is always out there to kick your butt.
—Mark Cuban.

When you are driving, if there is a dotted yellow line (white in some countries), you can pass or cross over into the other lane. However, if there is a solid yellow line, you cannot pass and you cannot cross over. Others cannot pass or cross over either. If you paint solid yellow lines around your priorities and the to-dos they contain, other priorities (what we call "lives") cannot pass or cross over. Another good way to look at it is as a solid yellow box. By compartmentalizing, you focus. When you operate within one boxed set of priorities, all six sides are solid yellow and you stay completely present-time conscious to the task at hand in that box. You can't step, look, or see outside a solid yellow box. You're forced to stay focused on what's in it and *only* what's in it.

If it's your devotional time with God, then you don't want to be thinking or looking at any other distraction. If you're on a date with a spouse, friend, or child, you don't answer cell phones, text, or check e-mail (tough to do these days). Instead you do something rarely done in a "busier-than successful" world: you focus!

The box causes you to completely direct your attention to your work, your spouse, your children, or your golf game so that you're thinking of nothing else. Maintaining solid, six-walled boxes makes you better at every one of your lives. Multitasking isn't really doing five things at once, because you can't think more than one thought at a time or do more than one thing at a time effectively. Your ability to focus on

a multitude of boxes in a brief window of time is a good definition of the effective new millennium multitasker!

SOLID YELLOW BOX EXAMPLES

Monday

6:30–7:00 a.m.: Devotional Life – Spiritual Growth Strategy

Your spiritual triathlon (put yourself in a solid yellow box with God)

7:10–7:19–:25 AM: Fitness Life – Healthy Lifestyle Strategy

Yes, I have a way for you to exercise and get in the shape of your life in nine to fifteen minutes!

9:00–1:00 p.m.: Financial Life (Work)

You put yourself in the yellow box of your chosen occupation. By focusing on your work and not your other lives, along with a dozen other distractions, you'll succeed and more than likely vastly improve your financial prospects. No other life is allowed in at that time. No personal calls, no exercise breaks, and no personal-growth reading during that time. Do not look at an unrelated e-mail.

1:15–2:15 p.m.: Saving lives outside – Social and Community Development

2:45–5:45 p.m.: Financial Life

6:30–9:00 p.m.: Family Life – Relationship Building Strategy

From 6:30 p.m. until 9:00 p.m., the whole family and each family member needs time. Now, by time, I don't mean throw everyone in front of the television and call it a jobwell done. This is especially difficult with bigger families, but it must be done. There's an impenetrable solid yellow family box with the group and with each individual. Again, you're in the box.

This means relational time—no television, no cell phones, no Internet. That makes it *quality* time. Plus, by making sure this time is written firmly in place consistently each day, it's also *quantity* time. If you want strong relationships and healthy children who don't grow up to quit college and take drugs, you need quality and quantity focused time to give yourself the best chance.

9:15–10:00 p.m.: Education time, Skill Sharpening, and/or Planning Strategy

The last hour before bed often becomes 3rd shift for an entrepreneur. Everyone is in bed and you can advance the mission further. I've written 17 books and most of them were written during this time.

A book or computer program designed to advance learning in an area important to the advancement of your personal life. This could also be time for relaxation or going to sleep. One hour a day, five days a week is two to three hundred hours of growing your mind and advancing your skills each year. Where will you be in ten years if you're consistently advancing your mind this way? Conversely, if all you fill that time with is reality television, where will your mind be in ten years? Plan your choice.

Not every minute has something in it, but ideally every "life" is scheduled. Sometimes it's nap life—but it's still scheduled. (We learned that one in kindergarten!) Certain "lives" happen every day, but others are strategically placed throughout the week so all of the items on the written to-do list are checked off and done well.

EMERGENCIES–OR ARE THEY?

Obviously, it doesn't always work out to the minute. Sometimes a child wakes up at 5:00 a.m. or there's a legitimately urgent matter. Just be "wise"—not everything is an emergency. Much of what you or others consider to be an emergency can actually be handled during the appropriate "life."

FLEXIBILITY

When something truly knocks you off schedule, practice flexibility. Remember: blessed are the flexible, for they shall enjoy life. However, work to get it all back on track as soon as you can.

IF YOU'RE MARRIED – START HERE:

Ask your spouse or significant other what they need from you and if there are kids; what they think the children need from you.

On the other hand, spouses need to respect their partner's mission. If you have a wife or husband living on purpose, be good to your wife or husband on purpose. The time that is not planned to be given to family should be free for to be used to provide and protect the family and to save the world.

Lives are like the rows of flowers in a garden. They need nourishment and attention. If you have a family, time needs to be allotted for the whole family unit, individual time for each family member needs to be considered, and the children's lives all need to be scheduled too. Families need a variety of different "lives" just to interact with each other.

There are family date times, which are times spent together as a family (*not* watching television—I repeat for emphasis).

You also need to box in date times with each child and your spouse. Date times are fun or organized teaching times that are one-on-one time spent together. Children also have activities that have to be scheduled into your lives, as well as organized for them to also start living lives with a future. These may include sports teams, homework, music lessons, games, parties, and personal growth time. While grades and athletic achievements are great, how much more important are spiritual achievements. Approach faith intentionally. Plugging in opportunities for your children to grow in the Lord should get more of your attention than As or points scored. Husbands and wives need to consult with each other to see how the time can be spent most equitably each week in order for each family member to feel like their needs—especially their relational needs—are being met.

CHILDREN'S PLAN

Here's an example of what a child's solid yellow boxes for a week might look like:

Normal Weekdays

7:00–7:15 a.m.: Devotional Time

4:00–5:30 p.m.: School Life

Including schoolwork, reading, and educational videos

6:00–7/8:00 p.m.: Play Life

Box out technology time. Today's youth can be headed towards no goals and with no rudder as they focus all or most of their efforts on text, YouTube, Instagram, and video games.

Monday, Wednesday, Friday

3:00–4:00 p.m.: Sports Life (E.g., baseball practice, train for a sport)

Thursday nights, Saturday and Sunday afternoons

Times vary: Family Life

Saturday

Noon–1:00 p.m.: Hobby or Music Life (E.g., piano lessons)

Remember: your child cannot be more organized or manage his life better than you do from the example you set!

WAR PLAN TIPS

You know you're in trouble when ...

... your war plan isn't determining how you spend the week and days.

... you're not looking at the war plan before making time decisions.

... you have not updated the war plan. If you haven't, chances are good that people are losing out.

... you don't reset your war plan weekly to adapt to change.

... you assume you're fine and you don't need the Battle Strategies. Skip, for example, date nights, fitness, and planning for your team meetings and rest assured- rough waters ahead!

STEPPING INTO GREATNESS

Eliminate with a chainsaw *everything t*hat doesn't belong and you w*ill s*culpt out a future *that honors God* . Do not accept that your life is irreparably busy. Lop off anything that isn't necessary for the life of your dreams. How do you start cutting? Ask yourself this question, "If I only had two hours a week to get things done, what would I focus all of my energy on?" Everything else is a candidate for the cut list. Plus, imagine how you would profit if you focused on the small group of things that really make the most difference to your present and your future.

DELEGATION ADDS EVEN MORE TIME

Many of my lives have details I delegate to someone else. I don't cut my grass, build my own deck, fix anything that breaks, order supplies at my office, do my own taxes, or change my own oil. The more I can pass on to someone else, the more time I have to go from $0 to $1 million.

Delegation also dramatically speeds up results. Not only am I more effective at the life I am living, but there are several other people helping me to move the other lives I have *forward*. So while I am being an author, a team of people is helping my lecture series grow and my clinic run smoothly.

All the people I delegate to have my schedule so they know when they can call me. People helping me with the details of my Author Life know to leave a message or e-mail me when I am in my Doctor Life. We speak or meet at set times throughout the week that are designated Author Life times. The accountants and managers in charge of business issues send me daily and weekly reports and updates to keep me abreast of what is happening. I then read these items and/or meet with these people only during designated Business Life times weekly or monthly. When I first try to get people to start delegating, I usually run into two problems:

Problem #1: The Control Freak

Many people have control issues, but some people have *huge* control issues. At some point in your life, you are going to have to trust somebody if you are ever going to take some weight off your back, reduce your stress, and move forward. Issues dealing with money, family, and important areas of your home or business may be hard for you to "let go" of, but you must learn to delegate even the vital things. It may take considerable time and prayer to find the right type of person, but there are a lot of high-quality, trustworthy people who need good jobs and would love to help you achieve your mission.

Problem #2: Penny-Smart and Dollar-Dumb

Understanding cost versus investment is another major reason people refuse to delegate. I hear things like "Why should I pay someone to mow my lawn (clean my house, paint my fence, do my taxes) when I can just do it myself?" This is called being "penny-wise and dollar-dumb." You save pennies and cost yourself thousands. While you are busy picking up socks, trimming hedges, and putting Armor All on your tires, you could be advancing your skills, growing your business, playing with your kids, or supporting your religious organization. You can easily spend several hundred hours a year working on "stuff" and "details" that you could have paid only pennies to someone else to accomplish for you. You could have used all that time to exponentially explode your life and construct a future to be proud of.

There are plenty of neighbors' kids who will cut your lawn for twenty dollars. If you cut your own lawn, you steal that kid's twenty dollars. You also steal time away from God, your family, and yourself.

Two are better than one, because they have a good return for their work: If one falls down, his friend can help him up. But pity the man who falls and has no one to help him up! — Ecclesiastes 4:9-10

HOME DELEGATION

My wife, Dr. Sheri, takes care of patients, is a mom, and has a very active fitness and spiritual life. We delegate parenting and other family responsibilities to each other whenever possible so we can both get our "lives" accomplished.

When our schedules clash at times, we delegate and get a babysitter or a grandma to help. We do this even if it is just a half hour to let her get a workout in or for me to be there if my wife and I want to pray or go for a run together.

For the success of your family and to help find prosperity in all areas, be sure to delegate at home.

THE ONLY LIFE I ALWAYS LEAD:

I Am Third:

1. God

2. Family

3. Me

When planning your time, God is first, your family is second, and your mission is third. However, this is not a vertical order. It is more horizontal, as if each of these parts of you were laid out on a table. The fact is, at the appropriate time, one of these three is a priority and deserves 100 percent of your undivided attention. If any are skipped or fail to receive the minimal amount of time required for success, life gets out of balance. Prioritizing is more working on the concept of compartmentalization than it is getting the order right from the top of the ladder on down.

Through compartmentalizing your life and delegating a tremendous amount of work, you become very time-efficient. You can live out multiple priorities with passion, excellence, and considerable productivity.

On the other hand, while you look to be very efficient with *time,* be careful not to be efficient with *God or people.* As a husband, dad, busy entrepreneur, and someone who is always seeking God, I have to constantly remind myself that God and other people come first—particularly the people closest to me whom I have the opportunity and responsibility to help. Therefore, I can never become subdued into thinking I am too busy achieving to stop and show my love and appreciation to God and the people who need *me.* God and people are the mission, along with the work!

God must be your *first* love. To show love for God, it is important to consider what He wants. I imagine God wants what most fathers would want. (Remember, this is your heavenly Father, so what He **wants** does not include more time fishing or lying on the couch watching football.) A father wants you to love Him, spend time with Him, and not get caught up in the bad things and useless distractions of the world. The Bible's word on this topic states, "Do not love the world or anything in the world. If anyone loves the world, the love of the Father is not in him" (1 John 2:15).

The people I work with or deal with every day are not a means to an end. I do all that I can to lead and encourage them and not just get something from them.

You can be efficient and economical with time, but you must be helpful and effective with people. *In every life you lead, God comes first, your family comes second, and you are third.* By blocking out days and daily time for God and family life, you help to prevent many of the emergencies.

FORGET TO PLAN, THEN PLAN TO FORGET

The reason they call it time "management" is because the word *management* implies some direct action that needs to be taken in order for your time to be actively "managed." For instance, to increase the need for repetitive physical movement or activity in your life, you don't just try to "squeeze in a workout" if time permits or you remember.

That is not managing your time; that is time managing you.

That is "managing" to let yourself off the hook when deadlines loom, meetings go late, you get hungry and feel rushed, you'll skip required fitness most if not every time.

If you want to start exercising regularly, you must cause-actively say, "At six in the morning on Monday, at five in the afternoon on Tuesday, and at six on Saturday night, I am exercising. That's it. Period. End of story." That way, you *cause* exercise to happen. It gets written in the book, and it's a done deal. Now you won't forget, and you'll stick to that plan.

You are finally managing your time.

Need to start eating better? Then don't start the week without some preparation. If you do, you will end up stuck at lunch and suddenly it's an emergency. You are starving, and the "Law of the Jungle" sets in, and all you are thinking about now is *survival.* The only place around you have time for is a fast-food chain or a convenience store, and instead of causing yourself to eat healthy, you end up reacting to your hunger emergency.

If you are going to start eating better, you have to plan it. You have to manage your time in order to find the time to make things work. You go shopping every Sunday, you cook for two or three days at a **time instead of one meal at time,** and you put some healthy food in containers that you can take to work with you. Then, when you are hungry, you already have healthy food right there next to you, and you can skip the candy bar or the cheeseburger.

You can't just try to figure out Mission Work when you get to it or try to remember it as you go. No matter what your situation, you need to start planning. Put it in the schedule, and stick to the schedule.

DON'T SMUDGE YOUR LINES

I'm convinced that about half of what separates the successful entrepreneurs from the non-successful ones is pure perseverance. —Steve Jobs, co-founder and CEO of Apple.

When following your War Plan, commit to doing each of the things you wrote down exactly as written. *Do not smudge your lines!* If you said you were going to jog a mile, three times per week, then jog a mile, three times per week. If you said you were going to make ten sales calls a day, then make at least ten sales calls per day. Do not skip or shortchange any part of your plan. If you do, you put reaching your goals in jeopardy.

Ability will never catch up with the demand for it. -Confucius.

As you put your war plan together and begin to fill it with the times that create progress, you wake up one day to find yourself a man or woman on a mission and on your way to a million.

SEIZE THE DAY!

Twenty years from now, you will be more disappointed by the things that you didn't do than by the ones you did do, so throw off the bowlines, sail away from safe harbor, catch the trade winds in your sails. Explore, Dream, Discover. -Mark Twain, author

I wish you Godspeed in your mission. I'm not sure how fast God-speed is for you. What I do know is that we need you. Whatever your calling is, it is eternally important to all of us.

In the movie Dead Poet's Society, Robin Williams looks at pictures in the trophy room of all of the heroes and teams of old and very eloquently tells us that we will all soon be "food for worms."

As the story goes, Ernest Hemingway was challenged to write a story that was less than ten words long. He wrote what is considered the saddest tale ever: "For sale, baby shoes, never worn."

Another author, Kurt Vonnegut, wrote, "In all the words of mice and men, the saddest are, 'What might have been.'" The poem never written, the song never sung, the plan of God's never hatched, the date that never happened, the potential never actualized, and the mission never fulfilled are all sad words indeed–but they do not have to be yours. Let that be others, but not you.

Your days on earth are numbered. So isn't it a shame that you put so many things off? You get so caught up paying your bills, trying to get somewhere on time, and handling your latest crisis that you forget to live. Out of fear of the consequences, endless distractions, or procrastination you do not grab for the things you really want and that really matter. The dreams you once had slowly fade away along with your health, your energy, and enthusiasm for life, until one day you find yourself trudging through the desert of despair, choking on the sand of your own regret.

To end on a much happier note, in the same movie Robin Williams says that we must "Carpe Diem," or "Seize the Day." I have laid out enough motivation and inspiration, and a map, to create, launch, and sustain a mission. I am also here to help you be the one that succeeds. If you are committed to your mission, I am committed to you. I would love to hear from you and find out where you need help going from zero to a million—and beyond. You can find me at drbenlerner. com or email me at doctorbenlerner@gmail.com.

Have fun saving the world!

– Dr. Ben

www.ingramcontent.com/pod-product-compliance
Lightning Source LLC
Chambersburg PA
CBHW021929190326
41519CB00009B/964